THE REFRACTIVE THINKER®

AN ANTHOLOGY OF DOCTORAL WRITERS

VOLUME XVI

Generations
Strategies for Managing Generations in the Workforce

Edited by Dr. Cheryl A. Lentz

THE REFRACTIVE THINKER® PRESS

The Refractive Thinker®: An Anthology of Higher Learning
Vol. XVI: Generations: Strategies for Managing Generations
in the Workforce

The Refractive Thinker® Press
www.RefractiveThinker.com
blog: www.DissertationPublishing.com

Please visit us on Facebook and like our Fan page.
www.facebook.com/refractivethinker

Books are available through The Refractive Thinker® Press at special discounts for bulk purchases for the purpose of sales promotion, seminar attendance, or educational purposes. Special volumes can be created for specific purposes and to organizational specifications. Please contact us for further details.

Individual authors own the copyright to their individual materials.
The Refractive Thinker® Press has each author's permission to reprint.

Copyright © 2019 by The Refractive Thinker® Press
Managing Editor: Dr. Cheryl A. Lentz • DrCherylLentz@gmail.com

Library of Congress Control Number: 2013945437

BUSINESS & ECONOMICS / Management & Leadership

Print ISBN: 978-1-73293-822-9
*Kindle and electronic versions available

Refractive Thinker® logo by Joey Root; The Refractive Thinker® Press logo design by Jacqueline Teng; cover design and production by Gary A. Rosenberg.

Printed in the United States of America

10   9   8   7   6   5   4   3   2   1

Contents

Testimonials

Clarissa Burt

CEO/Founder of *In the Limelight Media, LLC*
https://www.inthelimelightmedia.com

Learning doesn't always happen in a formal classroom; sometimes one learns from the school of hard knocks and experience, often in serving others. *The Refractive Thinker®* series looks to connecting these two worlds of business and learning. A refractive thinker® is one who never settles for anything less than everything, daring to dream a bit with a model to change the world of academic publishing by understanding the value of education and research—whatever its source. No one benefits from playing small, particularly regarding the needs of the various generations now working together in the marketplace. Refractive thinkers play on a big stage, truly desiring to change their world and ours. Join them.

Brian Jud

Executive Director of the Association of Publishers for Special Sales, author of 14 books including *How to Make Real Money Selling Books*
http://www.bookmarketingworks.com/

Authors always want to know the latest out-of-the-box strategy to sell more of their books. *The Refractive Thinker®* series adopts this innovative-thinking approach, so you can get your doctoral research out of academia and into the hands of those who need it. This volume, regarding the field of managing generations in the workforce, is a particularly good example of how to make that happen. There is no need to go it alone. Join your colleagues on a journey in search of creative and unique solutions as you navigate the landscape of business.

Martha Hanlon

CEO and Founder of Wide Awake Business
https://www.wideawakebusiness.com

Today more than ever before, multiple generations work side-by-side in every business imaginable. For leaders and managers, it demands new ways of developing a culture and management style that works for people motivated by radically different things. Most management books offer insights for what works for the current generation(s). But it's a trying task to find experts sharing proven strategies to improve leadership for up-and-coming generations such as Generation Y and Z? *The Refractive Thinker®* closes this hole in our vision and knowledge through its latest publication, *Vol XVI: Generations: Strategies for Managing Generations in the Workforce*. Regardless of your industry, you'll uncover insights to apply to your business based on current research findings on what is working for these newest additions to the workforce. No more head scratching. Now we have the resource to close our knowledge and action gap. The anthology approach insures different perspectives and approaches to open your mind to the possible.

Olivia Parr-Rud, MS

LOVE. Make It Your Business. Expert Data Scientist, Bestselling and Award-winning author, Corporate Love Ambassador, Self-Love Advocate, Author of *LOVE@WORK* and *The LOVE@WORK Method*™
http://www.LoveMakeItYourBusiness.com

In our increasingly complex global economy, business success depends on an agile, cohesive workforce. Human capital expenditures dominate the corporate budget. Workers from their early 20s to their late 80s and beyond are blending their skills and expertise to fuel innovation and drive profits. Today more than ever, there is a need to understand and leverage the talents of every generation. *The Refractive Thinker*® series offers powerful, practical insights and strategies for navigating our increasing complex business landscape. The blend of academic rigor with real world applications through the lens of refractive thinking strategies provides unique, cutting-edge solutions. *The Refractive Thinker*®: *Vol XVI: Generations: Strategies for Managing Generations in the Workforce* is a potent addition to this series as it offers powerful insights into hiring and managing talent across generations. Every business should make this entire series a staple in their corporate library.

"That is no vision of a distant millennium.
It is a definite basis for a kind of world attainable
in our own time and generation."

—Franklin Delano Roosevelt

The Power of Leadership

"In the end, our own success will be measured by the accomplishments that we have helped create in others."
—Dr. Greg S. Reid

Each generation brings their unique style to share their gifts with the world. With millennials in particular, this new generation asks us to challenge what we know, to really think in ways no other generation has of yet to solve new problems we face. They bring fresh perspective, with a new way of looking at things, particularly in this digital age. Yes, new generations will shake things up a bit and that's a good thing to get us all out of our comfort zones. If you change the way you think, your life changes.

As I speak with amazing and successful business leaders around the world as part of continuing the legacy of The Napoleon Hill Foundation, the question I ask them is why is this leadership thing so darn hard? Their answer? Successful leaders will tell you that people just don't like change. Even if change puts us in a better place—we resist. Yet what we resist, persists. If we don't change, then nothing changes. If you've done what you've always done, then you get what you've always got.

The secret is in discovering how to persevere through challenges to see change as an opportunity and as a gift. Successful leaders will tell you to feel the fear and do it anyway. Capitalize on the change. Do what others won't.

Successful leaders will tell you that it isn't that they don't feel fear; they simply recognize fear as part of the equation for success to persevere in spite of the challenges. Sometimes the challenges actually help to find a new and better way forward. This is a good thing. Success comes from sticking it out or stickability—to get to this better place. Successful leaders don't run from challenges; they run towards them. And they help others along the way.

Change may require a new way of thinking at times, but leadership fundamentals remain the same. Regardless of the generation, fundamentals are fundamentals. Leadership. Perseverance. Flexibility. Adaptability. Ethics. Character. Attitude. And yes even gratitude—gratitude for the challenges that often show us exactly where we need to be to find a new way forward—if and only if— we are willing to accept the challenge.

Life is easy when things go right. Our character is all about how we show up when they don't. Successful business is more about mindset, than what you do or to what generation you belong. Believe in yourself. Find others to help guide you along the way; learn to help others along your way. Successful business leaders will tell you there is no reason you have to go it alone. Find a mentor to follow in their footsteps. Ask for their counsel and follow up and follow through.

Leading this new generation is not as different or as difficult as many may think. Sure Millennials embrace technology more than previous generations, but how cool is that? Different is not bad. ALL generations can learn from each other if we each recognize the gifts each brings to the table. Being different can be a great gift—if we know how to use it to benefit those around us. It isn't just about us.

This Refractive Thinker® series is all about the power of difference, particularly the power in asking the right questions in doctoral research, as by using this strategy, the right answers will come. Refractive thinkers® are all about thinking differently. Thinking is not just in or out of the box. Refractive thinkers® think beyond the box as scholars who understand the power of research in search of answers.

Join me and these doctoral scholars to learn more about the research behind these new generations in the focus of this next volume in this award winning series. Get to know these scholars as they learn about new generations. Learn to see the world through their eyes, yet still embracing the wisdom and counsel from the experiences of generations that came before them. Research doesn't live in a vacuum but continues to build on the wisdom of the collective. A refractive thinker never settles for what is; they look instead to see what could be.

For the scholars of this Vol XVI: Generations, their missions are many, from learning about effective leadership strategies, to reducing turnover, to cybersecurity, to the wonders of the entrepreneur in this new digital age. The thread that links all of us together is that successful leaders believe they can make a difference to help those in any generation as they go in search of answers.

In the words of Gandi, "Be the change you want to see in the world."

Sincerely,
Dr. Greg Reid
CEO/Founder of Secret Knock
http://www.secretknock.co/
Author of *Stickability and Tokens*

About the Author...

A highly sought after keynote speaker for corporations, universities, and charitable organizations, Dr. Greg S. Reid is a master storyteller—inspiring, uplifting and motivating you in to your greatness. Experiencing Dr. Greg S. Reid on stage is like a rollercoaster ride you'll never forget, with twists and turns that are guaranteed to ignite your senses, leaving you on your feet screaming for more.
https://www.bookgreg.com/

Preface

Welcome to the award winning Refractive Thinker® Doctoral Anthology Series. We are thrilled to have you join us for the 18th volume in the series (Vol II was published 3 times), *The Refractive Thinker®: XVI Generations: Strategies for Managing Generations in the Workforce.* Join us as we continue to celebrate the accomplishments of doctoral scholars from around the globe.

Our mission continues to be to get research off the coffee table, out of the Ivory Tower of academia, and into the hands of people who cannot only use but benefit from the many insights and wisdom found from doctoral research results and findings. The goal is to continue to bridge the gap from the halls of academia into the halls of the business world. *The Refractive Thinker®* series continues to offer a resource from the many contributing doctoral scholars as they offer their chapter summaries of doctoral research well beyond the boundaries of a traditional textbook. Instead, the goal for this series is to use refractive thinking strategies to push the boundaries beyond conventional wisdom and to explore the paths not yet traveled particularly in this evolving digital age.

As we move into Spring 2019, this peer-reviewed publication offers readers insights and solutions to various challenges in working with multiple generations in the workforce from Baby Boomers to Generations X, Y, and Z. Our hope is for you to find answers regarding these unique challenges managers and leaders face in finding effective strategies to help guide your efforts in the boardroom. Within these pages, scholars offer insights from healthcare to cybersecurity, workplace resiliency to managing turnover, the benefits of hiring those with autism, an in depth look at artificial intelligence and reviewing the educational model in our schools to find more effective ways forward.

This volume will continue to shape the conversation of future success in business to examine proven strategies for continued excellence and profitability that have come from the research and pens of professional academicians and scholars around the world. The premise is to think not only *outside the box,* but also *beyond the box,* to create new solutions, to ask new questions, to proceed forward on new roads not yet explored or traveled. Our premise is to review academic research in a simple to digest executive summary format to offer new ways for business leaders to think about effective practices for strategies in their business based on what new research has to offer specifically growing the future of business.

With this volume, we continue to include a section to the series where Dr. Cheryl Lentz, *The Academic Entrepreneur,* concludes each chapter from a business point of view to link this doctoral research to applications for your business.

Remember, not only does *The Refractive Thinker®* series offer a physical book, we offer eBooks (Kindle, Nook, and Adobe eReader), and eChapters (individual chapters by author) that highlight the writings of your favorite Refractive Thinker® scholars, available through our website: http://www.RefractiveThinker. com, as well as www.Amazon.com . Be sure to also visit our social media to include our Facebook page, Twitter, our YouTube Channel, and our profile and groups on LinkedIN® for further discussions regarding the many ideas presented here.

We look forward to your continued support and interest of the more than 160 scholars within *The Refractive Thinker®* doctoral community who contributed to this multi award winning anthology series from around the globe. Our mission that began with Volume 1 many years ago is to bring research out of academia for application in the world of business to provide answers to the many questions asked.

Acknowledgments

The foundation of scholarly research embraces the art of asking questions—to validate and affirm, what we do, and why. Through asking the right questions, the right answers are found. Leaders often challenge the status quo, to offer alternatives and new directions, to dare to try something bold and audacious, to try something that has never been tried before. This 18th publication of our beloved 16-time award winning *Refractive Thinker*® series required the continued belief in this new publishing model, of a peer-reviewed doctoral anthology, by those willing to continue forward on this voyage.

We are grateful for the help of many who made this collaboration possible. First, let me offer a special thank you to our **Peer Review Board**, to include Dr. Joseph A. Gioia, Dr. Ron Jones, and myself; and our Board of Advisors to include Brian Jud and Dr. Jody Sandwisch; and media consultant / partner, Rebecca Hall-Gruyter and her amazing team.

My gratitude extends with a well-deserved thank you to our production team: Gary Rosenberg (production specialist) and Joey Root, designer of the original Refractive Thinker® logo.

Thank you. We appreciate everyone's contributions to this scholarly collaboration.

Job well done!

My best to our continued success!

Dr. Cheryl Lentz
Managing Editor and Chief Refractive Thinker®

CHAPTER 1

Millennial Indemnity to Ensure Leaders for Tomorrow: #LaisseznotLazy

Dr. Mark J. Tarmann, Jr.

The insurgence of Millennial employees is upon us. Specifically, the growing Millennial intricacies that current infrastructures and respective leaders are now trying to address. The complexities of Millennial employees created a need for leaders to develop effective management strategies and leadership succession plans. A plausible source of Millennial complexity is that Millennials more than prior generations' have grown up in conditions dictated by not only proximal societal and environmental norms but also world norms made readily available through technological advancements. With the surge of technological progress at a young age, Millennials have developed expectations of immediate gratification and have endured micro-management by parents and various leaders. All of which have contributed to Millennial employees having fragile psychological contracts with employers, a lack of job embeddedness, and increased mobility in comparison to their predecessors. Under the premise of #LaisseznotLazy, the objective of this chapter is to help *generational leaders,* those managing workforces composing of employees from various generations, address the problem that some organizations lack formal leadership succession plans to indemnify them against the disruptive complexities of Millennial employees. This chapter provides information that will empower leaders through *refractive thinking* to ensure leadership succession through the application of risk management practices to Millennial employee leadership. Refractive thinking is when someone can see potential in modifying traditional thinking through untraditional thinking to foster beneficial change (Lentz, 2009). More specifically, to help *generational leaders* strengthen Millennial psychological contracts, increase job embeddedness, and develop formal leadership succession to ensure leaders for tomorrow.

#Laisseznotlazy is a metaphoric hashtag homophone hashtag, based on the themes identified in the qualitative work in Tarmann (2017), that denotes the ideal management style for Millennial employee development, retention, and eventual leadership succession and encompasses the sentiments behind Millennial rebelliousness against current social and professional constructs. The hashtag makes information about the growing duel between the efforts of leaders to attract and retain Millennials long-term versus increased Millennial mobility easier to locate, which is imperative as Millennial continue to compose a more significant portion of the existing and incoming workforce. Tarmann (2017) identified an effective means of developing Millennial employees for succession planning in small to medium-sized enterprises. The basis of the Tarmann (2017) study and this chapter is to help *generational leaders* mitigate and indemnify themselves from the risks associated with the leadership of Millennial employees; being increased mobility and an increased rate of voluntary turnover. The chapter is structured to answer qualitative inquiries about Millennials, leadership succession, and development strategies appropriate for Millennial employee retention.

Who Are Millennials?

The offspring of Baby Boomers, Millennials are the most significant generational group since their parents (Debevec, Schewe, Madden, & Diamond, 2013). Millennial literature on generational differences supports occupational and commitment shifting in this young generation now entering the workforce (Lyons & Kuron,

2014). Of significance, is a generational shift in the environments that Millennials have grown and developed. For Millennials, born in or after 1991 and those in the workforce ranging from 23 to 35, growing up occurred in an environment flooded with significant technological advancements (Bolton et al., 2013, Devaney, 2015). In contrast, for prior generations, the settings in their nearest proximity set the norms, actions, and limitations associated with their characters. But, as a result of rapid technological advances after 1990, Millennials have had an ever-expansive opportunity to experience a world not made readily available to their predecessors. Key technology events were the new millennium Y2K and the mass digitalization of information (Cutler, 2015). Under the influence of the Internet, Millennials have grown up in an age exposed to global versus regional partners (Debevec et al., 2013). Because Millennials have experienced an inundation of immediately accessible information, worldwide liberties, and the development of a possible need for immediate gratification their respective work values, perceptions of established norms, and increased mobility have placed a *generational leader's* ability to develop a pipeline of experienced leaders at risk.

Why Are Millennials So Disruptive?

Millennial employees' have a decreased level of respect for the predominantly hierarchal structures that exist in the current corporate environment (Rodriguez & Rodriguez, 2015). Moreover, Millennials prefer a never experienced before the requirement for ease of accessibility to and clarity in communication by leadership (Rodriguez & Rodriguez, 2015). Millennials perceive the established industrial progressions of tasks, training, and advancement as archaic, which was evident in a micro-study conducted by Tarmann (2017). The qualitative evidence was supportive of the notion that Millennials are continuously seeking justification for the continued use of organizational processes established before the abundance of available and digitized information at their fingertips. Prior tasks and or skills learned through repetition under the tutelage of a senior mentor are now a "click" away on video streaming services such as YouTube. Thus, making *generational leaders* have to take into consideration preexisting short-term and long-term employee developments plans.

Unlike prior generations, Millennial employees have emphasized maximizing leisure and health, even at the sacrifice of higher incomes (Rodriguez & Rodriguez, 2015). The emphasis on working to live versus living to work has resulted in a conflict between current leadership evaluation and reward practices and the expectations of Millennial employees. Winter and Jackson (2015) stated that leadership would need to embrace how Millennial employees seek a work-life balance. As well as the accompanying sense of entitlement. An elevated sense of entitlement by Millennials that comes with an expectation for higher economic rewards (Leveson & Joiner, 2014). But also, a higher incidence of depersonalization. Depersonalization occurs when employees perceive that a leader or organization has removed that individuals' sense of individualism (Lu & Gursoy, 2016). Both entitlement and heightened depersonalization vulnerability in combination with an emphasis on leisure and health and the resulting increase in mobility are highly disruptive. To indemnify themselves against these risks, *generational leaders* face the task of developing a pipeline of experienced Millennial employee while emphasizing the individualistic attention Millennial employees feel entitled to while avoiding catalyst for depersonalization.

Where Are Millennials Going?

The organizational tenure of workers from prior generations in the workforce is more than three times that of Millennial employees (U.S. Department of Labor, 2014). Which asks the question, "Where are Millennial employees going?" Prestia, Dyess, and Sherman (2014) found that 78% of the current Millennial workforce seek new employment opportunities within two years of initial employment. With each transition, organizations incur the loss of viable leadership succession opportunities, lost capital investments in human capital, and the necessity to start the attraction, hiring, development, and retention cycle again. Ertas (2015) found Millennial employees have not only a higher rate of mobility but higher incidences on nonlinear career paths than their predecessors. These findings support the notion that the growing dominance of Millennial employees is bringing a generational workforce that favors a work-life balance.

Johnson and Ng (2016) attributed the higher incidence of impatience and job change by Millennials to an increased pursuit of higher education accomplishments. These accomplishment pursuits are in line with the entitlement associated with Millennial employees. Alternatively, Laird, Harvey, and Lancaster (2015) attributed the increased mobility to a misalignment between current evaluative and reward-based initiatives cemented in modern corporations and the confidence and entitlement values currently held by Millennial employees. Both are ideologies highlight the presence of a disconnection between current organizational leaders and Millennial employees. Haider et al. (2015) stated that financial incentives alone cannot guarantee commitments and that leaders must seek to increase tenure by aligning organizational ambitions with that of Millennial employees. Therefore, *generational leaders* are not only combatting a generation with a higher inclination for mobility than predecessors but a generation in which prior mitigative strategies are no longer effective.

Why Are Millennials Leaving?

The Tarmann (2017) study found that increased incidences of depersonalization and lack of established psychological contracts versus innate characteristics are why millennial employees are voluntarily separating from employers at a higher rate than prior generations. Leaders of Millennial employees must emphasize the establishment of strong psychological contracts with Millennial employees in leadership succession plans (Clinton & Guest, 2014). The foundation of such agreements is the avoidance of depersonalization. Leadership succession planning that emphasizes the removal of an employee's sense of individuality (Lu & Gursoy, 2016) is counterintuitive to the relational and individualistic recognition expected by Millennial employees (Kim, 2015).

Unlike their predecessors, Millennials have a pre-disposition for fragile psychological contracts because of their nurturing. Odenweller, Booth-Butterfield, and Weber (2014) noted that the preponderance of interventions by parents of Millennials during incidences of increased difficulty resulted in Millennial employees having deficiencies in social interaction and heightened susceptibility to anxiety with a natural response of quitting. So, current relational based leadership and associated succession strategies may perpetuate Millennial employee deficiencies and contribute to the increase in voluntary turnover.

The underlying cognitive component is that the presence of fragile psychological contracts makes Millennials employees susceptible to shocks. Shocks are any sudden event that disrupts an employee's perceptions of the status quo (Holtom, Michell, Lee, & Inderrieden, 2005). The violation of an employee's established views also falls under the classification of a shock (Shipp, Furst-Holloway, Harris, & Rosen, 2014). Shocks are catalysts for Millennial employees to consider various constructs. Lee and Mitchell's unfolding model of voluntary turnover theorized that voluntary separation constructs included (a) bringing the employees attention to opportunities presents in the outside job market, (b) remove distractions present in the employee's daily routines that have masked the consideration of alternative employment options, and (c) force the employee to reconsider their commitment to their present employer (Davis, Trevor, & Feng, 2015). A central foundation of the unfolding model of voluntary turnover was an acknowledgment of the different and varied considerations employees undergo when they choose to leave an employer. *Generational leaders* need to consider this concept in any leadership succession planning but in particular when conceptualizing plans for Millennial employees.

Why Leaders Need to Insure to Ensure?

Given the transient nature of Millennial employees, *generational leaders* need strategies not only ensure future operations but to insure themselves and their respective organization against the adverse effects caused by the increased mobility of Millennials higher incidences of voluntary separation. Tarmann (2017) found that Lee's and Mitchell's (1994) unfolding model of turnover aligned best with findings on minimizing voluntary separation by Millennial employees. Moreover, Tarmann (2017) found prominent supportive qualitative data that laissez-faire leadership was the best leadership style to mitigate the peril of increased voluntary turnover by Millennial employees. Also, that self-governance was an effective talent management methodology to engage and retain Millennial employees and reduce the effects of depersonalization (Tarmann, 2017). Consequently, a core risk management strategy for leaders in light of the increased mobility of Millennial employees is to develop an effective leadership succession plan.

The sustainability of operations is the objective of any organizational leaders. Succession planning ensures that the necessary knowledge and resources remain after critical employees leave (Ghandi & Kumar, 2014). Two succession concepts exist—the succession of ownership and leadership succession. The succession of ownership is when the entirety of ownership of an organization is transferred to a successor (Bogdány et al., 2014). In contrast, leadership succession is a continual process of (a) identification of critical positions, (b) identification of competencies, and (c) the identification of succession management strategies (Ghandi & Kumar, 2014). The latter that *generational leaders* play a crucial role.

What is a Leader's Role in Succession Planning?

The successful continuity of operations relies heavily on the actions of existing leaders and their leadership styles to promote or detour the growth of an organization (Ghee, Ibrahim, & Abdul-Haim, 2015.) Cleary stated the success of an organization is dependent on the effectiveness of its leader. As cited in Northouse (2013) the central component of leadership is the ability to exert influence. Varying leadership styles do exist. However, Tarmann (2017) found that some alternative theories, like the leader-member exchange theory, to the unfolding model of voluntary turnover were not appropriate as a means of mitigating the frequency in which Millennial employees voluntarily separate from an employer.

The leader-member exchange theory (LMX) categorizes leader-subordinate by the degree of the relationship established (Bagger & Li, 2014.) Concerning Millennials, Harris, Li, and Kirkman (2014) found that high-level LMX relationship can mitigate turnover. However, Tarmann (2017) excluded LMX because Millennials pose dominant self-actualization tendencies that represent inherent disruptions in the employee and employer relationship. These inherent disruptions could result in the establishment of weak LMX relationships and perpetuate versus mitigate voluntary separation (Harris et al., 2014). Moreover, the LMX theory was the wrong lens to identify mitigating strategies to retain Millennial employees; also, that the identification of an appropriate leadership style is a critical component in the development of effective leadership succession plans.

Why Do Leaders Need Formal Leadership Succession Plans?

The sustainability of operations is presumably the prime objective of any organization and its leadership. The feasibility of such succession plans depends on the methods outlined in the procedures (Ghandi & Kumar, 2014). The methods employed for leadership succession are a crucial element. As the need for leaders to replace critical employees is a periodic and repetitive process just as is the need to evaluate succession planning routinely (Bogdány, Balogh, & Csizmadia, 2014). Unfortunately, many leaders struggle with evaluating succession planning regularly. As Lynch (2015) found, leaders' struggles arise from an inability to recruit, train, and manage others. When left to their own devices, the insufficiencies may lead to the cessation of operations, more prominently in family-run operations. Giarmareo (2015) found that 70% of family-run businesses studied ceased after the transference of leadership obligations from one generation to the next. Given the volatility of Millennial retention, organizational leaders can benefit from the development and establishment of formal leadership succession plans.

What Do Leaders Need to Have in Their Plans?

Leaders need leadership succession plans that have a combination of laisses-faire leadership elements and opportunities for Millennials to experience opportunities for self-governance to increase millennial employee retention within their organizations. As exemplified by the comments afforded by participating SME leaders in the Tarmann (2017) study, where the *generational leaders* stated, "We encourage our employees to think like entrepreneurs which has proven to very effective" and "Everybody (Millennials) needs to do things their own way. If you must tell them (Millennials) step-by-step, it increases aggravations. If the job gets finished, it should not matter what order or what way they (Millennials) get it done. So, a happy workplace is one where we do not put too much stress on Millennial employees." The leader's perception was that by minimizing interference and allowing their Millennial employees to experience accountability and establish their own norms for operating that the end result was a completed task just as it would have been with micro-management. As a result, the concept of laissez-faire leadership and self-governance are strategies of interest for *generational leaders.*

Why Do Leaders Need Laissez-Faire Leadership?

Fiaz, Su, Ikran, and Saqib (2017) found that laissez-faire leadership impacts employee motivation by minimizing disruptions. Simply stated, the laissez-faire leadership style reduces the occurrences of the shocks categorized by Lee's and Mitchell's (1994) unfolding theory of voluntary turnover. The leadership style is counter-intuitive as laissez-faire leadership principles seek leaders to take a passive role in the direction of human capital. However, the passive leadership style does offer flexibility and happiness when compared to alternative relational and transactional-based leadership practices. Leaders employing a laissez-faire leadership style can work in whatever boundaries an organization's culture and human capital dictate and perceives employees are self-sufficient (Fiaz et al., 2017, Wong & Geissner, 2015).

However, context is of importance. As aforementioned, Millennials have fragile psychological connections and incidences of self-entitlement. As a result, it is not inconceivable that those studies on Millennial employees that emphasize the necessity of continual direction and feedback have validity. An argument is that the flexibility afforded by the passivity of laissez-faire leadership enable a *generational leader* in transitioning from transactional, transformational, and handoff management to match the complexities of Millennial employees.

Just as evidence-based information supports micro-management of Millennials, scholars also found evidence in support passive leadership. Tarmann (2017) concluded that when Millennial employees experience minimal leadership intervention and oversight, as previously endured under helicoptering parents, the return was increased job embeddedness and mitigation of voluntary turnover by Millennial employees. Fiaz et al. (2017) found a positive correlation between a laissez-faire leadership style and employee morale and improved efficiency. Further supported by the SME leadership participant in the Tarmann (2017) study. When interviewed, the leaders of various SMEs that employed Millennials with at least 3 years of employment alluded to a circular surplus of human capital based on their leadership style. Specifically, that when leadership utilized laissez-faire or passive leadership styles, the leaders found a consistent flow of Millennials sought employment at the respective establishments. The leader's attributed the surplus to minimal incidences of disruption resulting in high employee morale and increased attractiveness for potential future hires. The conclusion being that *generational leaders* have to navigate the complexities of Millennial employee and indemnify themselves through an ability to transition from active to passive leadership afforded by a laissez-faire leadership style.

Why Do Leaders Need Millennials to Contribute?

The final mitigative component for millennial employee indemnification falls under the umbrella of talent management. Talent management for leadership succession planning is the development of employee pools to help current leaders fill essential positions when vacated (Ariss. Cascio, & Paauwe, 2014). Talent management enables leaders to develop human capital in line the organization strategic initiatives to maintain the infrastructure when positions are vacated (Collings, 2014). This issue for *generational leaders* is as predecessors begin to leave the development of useful succession pools of tenured millennials is being regularly circumvented by the increased Millennial employee mobility and lack of job embeddedness. As a result, leaders will need to draw upon the ability for talent management to increase employee motivation. Per Festing and Schafer (2014) a byproduct of talent management is motivation. To do so, leaders must recognize the utility of self-governance with millennial employees to increase motivation, exert social pressure, and strengthen fragile psychological contracts.

Millennial employees need opportunities for self-governance. Stewart et al. (2017) stated managers should be mindful of their Millennial human capital and be open to considerations of modifications to workplace culture and performance to increase retention. Self-governance places Millennial employees at the forefront of mitigating any applicable shocks to the status quo. Moreover, when Millennial employees are charged with overseeing any initiating events, managing behavioral responses, and task the self-actualization and accountable benefit the organization by re-affirming psychological contracts and increases job embeddedness. An additional SME leader in Tarmann (2017) summarizes this process the best when they stated, "When left to govern themselves, the employees (Millennials) seem to form their own hierarchies where employees progress into self-created leadership roles over time and in turn train incoming employees."

With each accomplishment obtained through self-efficacy, Millennial employees experience responsibility and accountability for success which plays to their sense of entitlement. Millennials also become aware of the necessary effort for success and thus generate the necessary and appropriate level of motivation. Purvis et al., 2015 stated that self-efficacy is a suitable means to exert the motivation force on an individual. In turn, the motivation force affects behavioral decisions (Chen, Ellis, & Suresh, 2016). Specifically, the motivational force mitigates the shocks and or catalyst that makes Millennial employees consider voluntarily separating from an employer.

Now that *generational leaders* can understand the necessity for formal leadership plans to indemnify themselves and their respective organizations from the complexities of Millennial employees. It is an appropriate Segway to conclude with the recommendation on how to put the metaphorical Millennial employee insurance plan together.

Putting It All Together

The reality is that a more significant number of organizations and its leaders either lack leadership succession plans or have plans that are inadequate to address those characteristics associated with Millennial employees. The consolidation and application of concepts expressed in this chapter will aid *generational leaders* in the composition of updated and formal leadership succession plans to metaphorically insure themselves through the mitigation of millennial employee complexities as the generation continues to become a growing presence in the workforce. To encourage leaders to ensure future sustainability through the reduction of cognitive shocks as defined by Lee and Mitchells (1194) unfolding model of voluntary turnover. To do so, leaders need to be conscious of the fragility of the psychological contracts Millennial employees establish with leadership and their high susceptibility to incidences of depersonalization. That a leader should not be a substitute for the parent that used micromanagement in the nurturing of Millennial children but capitalize on principles of laissez-faire leadership to maximize situational leadership variance to match that of Millennial employee leadership needs. Finally, to successfully manage talent, a leader needs to capitalize on the generate motivational force on the behavioral decisions of Millennial employees by enabling and empowering the Millennial employees with opportunities to be self-sufficient.

Conclusion

Generational disruptiveness, especially in the workplace, will continue well after the rise and retirement of the Millennial generation. However, Millennials currently represent the first generation in which the rate of technological advancement, access to information, and decreased dependency on organizations for enrichment have lowered levels of job embeddedness and increased the frequency of voluntary turnover. Simultaneously, Millennials place greater emphasis on establishing a work-life balance, social transparency, and rebellion against what they perceive to be outdated industrial operations and development. The purpose of this chapter was to empower *generational leaders* through refractive thinking on how to strengthen psychological contracts, increasing job embeddedness, and developing effective leadership succession plans to insure and indemnify themselves, metaphorically, against the transient nature of Millennial employees. Specifically, the employment of practices to create and continually evaluate formal leadership succession plans, employ elements of laissez-faire or passive leadership, and by providing Millennial employees opportunities to self-govern themselves and capitalize on motivational forces in the management of Millennial employee talent to ensure future operations.

THOUGHTS FROM THE ACADEMIC ENTREPRENEUR

The problem to be solved:

- Some organizational leaders lack formal leadership succession plans to leaders insure their respective organizations against the increased mobility of Millennial employees

The goals:

- The goal is to Empower generational leaders on how to developing effective leadership succession plans that strengthen psychological contracts, minimize cognitive shocks, increasing job embeddedness, and exert motivational force on Millennial employee behavior to ensure future operations.

The questions to ask:

- Has my organization established or updated leadership succession plans in anticipation of hiring additional Millennials and the quickly approaching retirement of Baby Boomers?
- What is my current leadership style and is it the best suited to lead Millennials?

Today's Business Application:

- Effective leaders who understand the mobility associated with Millennials and poses flexibility in their respective leadership style are better equipped to respond successfully to shocks and minimize catalysts of a Millennial employee's cognitive pathways in consideration of voluntary turnover.
- Formality is fundamental to leadership succession plans to prevent or lessen the effects or reliance on reactive or micro-managerial leadership styling tendencies.
- Continuous evaluation of formal plans to affirm the presence of self-actualization, accountability, and engagement of the entrepreneurial mindset of Millennial employees will help leaders to strengthen psychological contract and increase job embeddedness by Millennials.

REFERENCES

Ariss, A., Cascio, W. F., & Paauwe, J. (2014). Talent management: Current theories and future research directions. *Journal of World Business, 49,* 173-179. doi:10.1016/j.jwb.2013.11.001

Bagger, J., & Li, A. (2014). How does supervisory family support influence employees' attitude and behaviors? A social exchange perspective. *Journal of Management, 40,* 1123-1150. doi:10.177/0149206311413922

Bogdány, E., Balogh, Á., & Csizmadia, T. (2014). Leadership succession and the origin of successor in Hungarian SMEs. *Management & Marketing, 9,* 283-300. Retrieved from http://www.managementmarketing.ro

Bolton, R. N., Parasuraman, A., Hoefnagels, A., Migchels, N., Kabadayi, S., Gruber, T., & . . . Solnet, D. (2013). Understanding Generation Y and their use of social media: A review and research agenda. *Journal of Service Management, 24,* 245-267. doi:10.1108/09564231311326987

Chen, L., Ellis, S. C., & Suresh, N. (2016). A supplier development adoption framework using expectancy theory. *International Journal of Operations & Productivity Management, 36,* 592-615. doi:10.1108/ijopm-09-2013-0413

Clinton, M. E., & Guest, D. E. (2014). Psychological contract breach and voluntary turnover: Testing a multiple mediation model. *Journal of Occupational & Organizational Psychology, 87,* 200-207. doi:10.1111/joop.12033

Collings, D. G. (2014). Integrating global mobility and global talent management: Exploring the challenges and strategic opportunities. *Journal of World Business, 49,* 253-261. doi:10.1016/j.jwb.2013.11.009

Cutler, N. E. (2015). Millennials and finance: The "Amazon Generation." *Journal of Financial Service Professionals, 69,* 33-39. Retrieved from http://fincialpro.org

Davis, P. R., Trevor, C. O., & Feng, J. (2015). Creating a more quit friendly national workforce?: Individual layoff history and voluntary turnover. *Journal of Business and Psychology, 30,* 137-147. doi:1037/ap10000012

Debevec, K., Schewe, C. D., Madden, T. J., & Diamond, W. D. (2013). Are today's millennials splintering into a new generational cohort? Maybe! *Journal of Consumer Behavior, 12,* 20-31. doi:10.1002/cb.1400

DeVanney, S. A. (2015). Understanding the millennial generation. *Journal of Financial Service Professionals, 69,* 11-14. Retrieved from http://financialpro.org

Ertas, N. (2015). Turnover intentions and work motivations of millennial employees in federal service. *Public Personal Management, 44,* 401-423. doi:10.1177/00910260155881993

Festing, M., & Schafer, L. (2014). Generational challenges to talent management: A framework for talent retention based on the psychological-contract perspective. *Journal of World Business, 49,* 262-271. doi:10.1016/j.jwb.2013.11.010

Fiaz, M., Su, Q., Ikram, A., & Saqib, A. (2017). Leadership styles and employees' motivation: Perspective from an emerging economy. *Journal of Developing Areas, 51*, 143-156. doi:10.1353/jda.2017.0093

Gandhi, D., & Kumar, P. (2014). Succession planning: Developing leaders for tomorrow to ensure organizational success. *International Journal of Business & Management, 2*, 1-5. Retrieved from http://www.theijbm.com

Ghee. W. Y., Ibrahim, M. D., & Abdul-Haim, H. (2015). Family business succession planning: Unleashing the key factors of business performance. *Asian Academy of Management Journal, 20*, 103-126. Retrieved from http://web.usm.my/aam

Giarmareo, J. (2012). The three levels of family business succession planning. *Journal of Financial Service Professionals, 66*, 59-69. Retrieved from http://financialpro.org

Haider, M., Rasli, A., Akhtar, S., Yusoff, R.B. M., Malik, O.M., Aamir, A., . . . & Tariq, F. (2015). The impact of human resource practices on employee retention in the telecom sector. *International Journal of Economics and Financial Issues, 5*, 63-69. doi:10.9790/487x-16167681

Harris, T. B., Li, N., & Kirkman, B. L. (2014). Leader-member exchange (LMX) in context: How LMX differentiation and LMX relational separation attenuate LMX's influence on OCB and turnover intentions. *Leadership Quarterly, 25*, 314-328. doi:10.1016/j.leaqua.2013.09.001

Holtom, B., Mitchell, T. R., Lee, T. W., & Inderrieden, E. J. (2005). Shocks as cause of turnover: What they are and how organizations can manage them. *Human Resource Management, 44*, 337-352. doi:10.1037/mil0000055

Johnson, J. M., & Ng, E. S. (2016). Money talks or millennials walk: The effect of compensation on nonprofit millennial workers sector-switching intentions. *Review of Public Personnel Administration, 36*, 283-305. doi:10.1177/0734371x15587980

Kim, J. (2015). What increases public employees' turnover intention? *Public Personal Management, 44*, 496-519. doi:10.1177/0091026015604447

Liard, M. D., Harvey, P., & Lancaster, J. (2015). Accountability, entitlement, tenure, and satisfaction in Generation Y. *Journal of Managerial Psychology, 30*, 87-100. doi:10.1108/JMP-06-2014-0227

Lee, Y. G., Bartkus, K. R., & Lee, M. (2015). The diversity of legacy motivation: Succession planning of African-American, Mexican-American, and Korean-American business owners. *American Journal of Entrepreneurship, 8*, 71-93. Retrieved from http://americanjournalentrepreneurship.org

Lentz, C. A. (2009). Preface. In C. Lentz (Series Ed.), *The refractive thinker*® *An anthology of higher learning: Vol. 2. Research methodology* (pp. xiv-xv). Retrieved from https://books.google.com

Leveson, L., & Joiner, T.A. (2014). Exploring corporate social responsibility values of millennial job-seeking students. *Education and Training, 56*(1), 21-34. doi:10.1108/ET-11-2020-0121

Lu, A. C. C., & Gursoy, D. (2016). Impact of job burnout on satisfaction and turnover intention do generational differences matter? *Journal of Hospitality & Tourism, Research, 40*, 210-235. doi:10.1177/1096348013495696

Lynch, M. (2015). Successful transitions: Getting it right. *Journal of Financial, Planning, 28*, 16-18. Retrieved from http://www.onefpa.org

Lyons, S., & Kuron, L. (2014). Generational differences in the workplace: A review of evidence and directions for future research. *Journal of Organizational Behavior, 35*, S139-S139-S157. doi:10.1002/job.1913

Northouse, P. G. (2013). *Leadership: Theory and practice* (6th ed.). Thousand Oaks, CA: Sage.

Odenweller, K. G., Booth-Butterfied, M., & Weber, K. (2014). Investigating helicopter parenting, family environments, and relational outcomes for millennials. *Communication Studies, 65*, 407-425. doi:10.1080/10510974.2013.811434

Prestia, A. S., Dyess, S. M., & Sherman, R. O. (2014). Planting the seeds of succession. *Nursing Management, 45*(3), 30-37. doi:10.1097/01. numa.0000443941.68503.09

Purvis, R. L., Zagenczyk, T. J., & McCray, G. E. (2015). What's in it for me?: Using expectancy theory and climate to explain stakeholder participation, its direction and intensity. *International Journal of Project Management, 33*, 3-14. doi:10.1016/j.ijproman.2014.03.003

Rodriguez, A., & Rodriguez, Y. (2015). Metaphors for today's leadership: VUCA world, millennial and "cloud leaders." *Journal of Management Development, 34*, 854-886. doi:10.1108/JMD-09-2013-0110

Ship, A.J., Furst-Holloway, S., Harris, T. B., & Rosen, B. (2014). Gone today but her tomorrow: Extending the unfolding model of turnover to consider boomerang employees. *Personal Psychology, 67*, 421-462. doi:10.1111/peps.12039

Stewart, J. S., Oliver, E. G., Cravens, K. S., & Oishi, S. (2017). Managing millennials: Embracing generational differences. *Business Horizons, 60*, 45-54. doi:10.1016/j.bushor. 201608011

Swartz, E., Amatucci, F. M., & Coleman, S. (2016). Using a multiple method and mixed mode approach to examine women entrepreneur negotiating styles. *International Journal of Gender and Entrepreneurship, 8*, 48-68. doi:10.1108/ ijge-09-2013-0060

Tarmann Jr M. (2017). *Small to medium enterprise succession planning: Millennial employee development* (Doctoral dissertation). Retrieved from https://scholarworks.waldenu.edu

U.S. Department of Labor. (2014). *Employee tenure in 2014*. Retrieved from http://www.bls.gov

Winter, R. P., & Jackson, B. A. (2015). Work values preferences of Generation Y: performance relationship insights in the Australian public service. *International Journal of Human Resource Management*, 1-19. doi:10.1080/09585192.2015.1 102161

Wong, C. A., & Laschinger, H. K. S. (2015). The influence of frontline manager job strain on burnout, commitment and turnover intention: A cross-sectional study. *International Journal of Nursing Studies, 52*, 1824-1833. doi:10.1016/j.ijnurstu.2015.09.006

About the Author...

Dr. Mark Joseph Tarmann Jr. resides in the historic town of Williamstown, NJ. Dr. Mark, lovingly known as husband and father to his wife and son, is a claims analyst and adjunct instructor of risk management courses facilitated by the Insurance Institute in Malvern, PA, and adjunct professor with Cumberland County College in association with Rowan College for the newly created degree path in risk management. Dr. Mark is the innovator behind #LaisseznotLazy and Dr. Mark Presents featured on various social platforms including LinkedIn, www.insurancenerds.com, and Twitter. He has also been featured in various podcasts, minority leadership periodicals, and was a key note speaker at the Gamma Iota Sigma national conference in Chicago, IL.

Awards include: Designations for completed course work in General Insurance (AINS), Insurance Services (AIS), Personal Insurance (API), Claim Handling (AIC), Risk Management (ARM), and the highest accreditation in insurance the Charted Property Casualty Underwriter (CPCU) designation by the American Institute.

Dr. Mark Tarmann is also an active member of CPCU society, Philadelphia chapter.

Dr. Mark continues to strive to establish a legacy and contribute to society through public speaking, published works, teaching, and sharing his passion for millennial development and succession to ensure the longevity of talented human capital.

To reach Dr. Mark Joseph Tarmann Jr. for additional, please visit his **websites:** www.linkedin.com/in/marktarmannjr https://insnerds.com/insurance-speakers-com/ or **e-mail:** marktarmannjr@gmail.com

CHAPTER 2

Post-Millennial's Autistic Workers

Dr. Natalie Casale

According to Pew Research Center (2018b), the Silent and Greatest generations include people born 1945 or earlier, Baby Boomer generation is born 1946 to 1964, Generation X is born 1965 to 1980, Millennial generation is born 1981 to 1996, and Post-Millennial generation is born 1997 or later (no end date defined as of 2019). The Silent and Greatest generations declined in the U.S. labor force; approximately 3.7 million members employed in 2015 (Pew Research Center, 2018c). The Baby Boomer, Generation X, and Millennial generations make up about 50 million each (Pew Research Center, 2018c). In 2019, the oldest Post-Millennial generation is 21 (Pew Research Center, 2018b); the first to begin to enter the workforce.

Parallel to the beginning of the Post-Millennial generation as they consider work options and career choices, the number of persons diagnosed with autism spectrum disorder (ASD) continues to increase (Centers for Disease Control [CDC] and Prevention, 2018). In 1995 (end of the Millennial generation), the autism and developmental disabilities monitoring (ADDM) network identified 1 in 5000 children with autism (CDC and Prevention, 2018). In 1997 (the beginning of the Post-Millennial generation), the ADDM identified 1 in 110 children diagnosed with autism, a 600% increase since 1995 (CDC and Prevention, 2018). As of 2014, the number of children identified with autism was 1 in 59 children (CDC and Prevention, 2018).

An increase in autism (CDC and Prevention, 2018) with the

Post-Millennial generation will introduce a need for new strategies to help autistic people fit into the workforce. The refractive thinker will investigate the current strategies company leaders implemented to create a successful work environment and career opportunities for autistic people.

The focus of this chapter is to identify strategies an organizational leader can use to take advantage of the unique skills autistic workers have that will fit into the work environment. The specific problem is some leaders do not understand how an autistic worker's unique skills would benefit the organization. Autistic workers could use additional care to feel comfortable in the workforce as demonstrated by company leaders from SAP (Florentine, 2015; SAP, 2019), EY (Ernst & Young) (EY Global, 2018), Microsoft (Microsoft, 2019), and Freddie Mac (Freddie Mac, 2019). Understanding the benefits of hiring autistic workers and creating a comfortable workspace will benefit the worker and success of the company.

Who are the Post-Millennials?

People born 1997 or later (no end date defined as of 2019) are temporarily called Post-Millennials, the generation after Millennials (Pew Research Center, 2018b). Other interim names for this generation include Generation Z, Gen Z, iGen, or Centennials ("A Post Millennial," 2018). In this chapter, the term Post-Millennials or Post-Millennial generation identifies the people from the new generation analyzed.

The Post-Millennial generation includes people more diverse than the Millennial generation ("A Post Millennial," 2018). Differences in diversity include culture, religion, and sexual preferences ("747 Insights," 2018). According to 747 Insights (2017), 80% of Post-Millennials reported their peers are from different cultures, a significant increase from the Millennial generation.

Many Post-Millennials are multicultural and / or have parents of different sexes; therefore, are open-minded and accepting individuals (Pew Research Center, 2018b).

The Post-Millennials were too young or were born after the 9-11 terrorist attacks in the United States; therefore, those of this generation live in a life aware of terrorism, and the awareness of precautions and security checks to live in a safe environment ("A Post Millennial," 2018). Other violent events affecting this generation include global and local terrorist attacks, school shootings, sexual assaults, and cyber-bullying; therefore, the concern for safety is part of everyday existence and communicated in the media (Beck & Wright, 2019). Post-Millennials are quick to form social justice movements based on making a difference of the violence they are accustomed to witnessing (Seemiller & Grace, 2017).

Post-Millennials are more technically savvy than Millennials (Beck & Wright, 2019; Fratricova & Kirchmayer, 2018). Social media and mobile device usage are a common means of communication ("A Post Millennial," 2018). According to the Pew Research Center (2018a), 78% (398 of 507) of Post-Millennial elementary students use a tablet regularly. Beck and Wright (2019) questioned a 13-year-old who suggested her experience with a tablet or cell phone is better than conversing with actual people. Beck and Wright suggested Post-Millennials constantly connect with their peers through technology and devices; therefore, they are socially conscious and know how to get information quickly. They prefer media to share pictures and videos; therefore, they are more visual learners (Beck & Wright, 2019).

Post-Millennials in the Workforce

The oldest Post-Millennial is 21 as of 2019 (Pew Research Center, 2018b); therefore, members of this generation are old enough to enter the workforce. Most popular educational and career choices are in science, technology, engineering, and mathematics (STEM) because of everyday casual use and understanding of technology and devices (Beck & Wright, 2019). The Post-Millennial generational cohorts are conservative with money, are not risk takers, and are career conscious; therefore, they want to succeed in the workplace (Beck & Wright, 2019). Seemiller and Grace (2017) suggested Post-Millennials prefer short-term contracts as opposed to a long-term commitment to one company.

Fratricova and Kirchmayer (2018) concluded factors that hinder the work motivation for Post-Millennials include boredom with the content of work, negative team environment, heavy workload, and the feeling of no sense of purpose. Because of the impact of terrorism and other traumatic life experiences, community engagement motivates the Post-Millennial (Seemiller & Grace, 2017). Seemiller and Grace (2017) concluded Post-Millennials want firsthand learning experiences and opportunities to apply immediately what they learned; however, they would rather observe another employee perform the task before doing the work themselves.

Post-Millennials expect information to be authentic and communicated digitally; therefore, focus on emails and texting as the main source of communication (Beck & Wright, 2019). Post-Millennials can easily retrieve information with a click on a smart phone, tablet, or computer (Seemiller & Grace, 2017). Post-Millennials do not save information; they delete information regularly because of the daily usage of data they need to purge regularly, specifically from taking photos and videos for social media such as Instagram and Snapchat (Beck & Wright, 2019).

What is Autism?

Leaders willing to hire autistic workers need to understand the details of the disability, and the challenges and strengths adults experience. Autism, also known as ASD, is a disability most often diagnosed in children (Autism Society, 2016b). ASD, a neurodevelopmental disorder, challenges a child through adulthood the ability to communicate and socialize (Autism Society, 2016b). ASD has different forms. Issues with communication include a lack of social skills and interaction with others, and speech difficulties (Autism Speaks, 2019b). Other forms of ASD include repetitive behaviors and nonverbal communication (Autism Speaks, 2019b). According to Autism Speaks (2019b), ASD has many subtypes triggered by environmental and genetic factors.

Because ASD has many different patterns, the costs to treat the disease are significant. According to Autism Speaks (2019a), the treatment cost for one individual's lifetime is $2 million. This total does not include the $250,000 to raise a child in the United States (Ostrow, 2014). Costs to raise a child with autism include doctor care, specialists, medication, therapy, and special needs education (Autism Speaks, 2019a).

Children with autism have many challenges, but they also have strengths. A variety of strengths include independent thinking, loyalty, nonjudgmental listing, understanding rules and sequences, logical thinking, decisions making, skills in math, computer, music, and art, long-term memory skills, honesty, punctuality, and visual thinkers (Sabapathy et al., 2017). Because ASD has different forms (Autism Society, 2016b), people with autism will not have all strengths; however, a combination of strengths can prove beneficial in the workplace.

Although ADS is a neurodevelopmental disorder with many life challenges for the autistic child or adult, the disease does not limit the autistic adult's ability to work. Autistic individuals have talents that would thrive in the workplace. However, understanding the disability and the challenges ADS presents will create a successful work environment and career for the autistic individual.

Autistic Workers

The increase in autism created a new concern for jobs available for autistic adults. In 2017, 35% (240 of 680) of autistic adults attended college; 85% (192 or 240) cannot find employment (Autism Society, 2016a). The unemployment rate for all people completing college is 4.5% (Bureau of Labor Statistics, 2019); therefore, a significant difference for those with autism earning degrees with nowhere to work resulting in the potential inability to afford to live independently. Compare this fact to the number of Post-Millennials diagnosed with autism; company leaders should consider what skills autistic workers can bring to the company's success.

Autistic adults have proven to have a variety of skills they excel in the workplace, such as retaining information, attention to detail, mathematical concepts, coding; logical and analytical skills used for software testing, and ability to focus for long periods of time (Nicholas, Mitchell, Dudley, Clarke, & Zulla, 2018). According to the Autistic Self Advocacy Network (2019), autistic individuals think differently. Understanding these differences can help the autistic person adjust to a safe work environment and benefit the company goals. For example, people with autism can work well in a routine because they adapt quickly to repetitive movement (Autistic Self Advocacy Network, 2019).

Post-Millennials with autism want financial independence; therefore, may desire to attend college and find jobs to live on their own (Sosnowy, Silverman, & Shattuck, 2018). Young adults with autism, studied by Sosnowy et al. (2018), indicated colleges need to provide support and services to meet their disability challenges. The parents of the studied individuals indicated their children were emotionally satisfied with accomplishments from higher education and employment; however, accepted work after college that did not pay as well as someone without autism (Sosnowy et al., 2018). The parents also stated their autistic young adult as overqualified and bored with the jobs accepted after college (Sosnowy et al., 2018).

Brooke et al. (2018) studied what inspires employees with autism to long-term employment. Brook et al. concluded companies that offer programs with constant assessments and frequent support provide the services to work toward long-term employment. Other benefits include seeking positions that meet the individual's skills, other opportunities within the company, and promotions (Brook at al., 2018). Wadsworth, Nelson, Rossi, and Hill (2016) concluded assigning a mentor to the autistic worker, preferably familiar with ASD, would provide ease with training and asking questions about work. Company leaders who develop programs designed to assist the autistic worker will help the individual adjust to the work environment.

Autism Friendly Employers

Several company leaders recognize the unique talent and skills autistic adults can bring to the work process. Companies, such as SAP (Florentine, 2015; SAP, 2019), EY (EY Global, 2018), Microsoft (Microsoft, 2019), and Freddie Mac (Freddie Mac, 2019) created programs for those with ASD. There are similarities and differences between these programs; however, the results are the same–to provide an autistic adult employment opportunity, regardless of their generation.

SAP (System Applications and Products) developed a program titled Autism at Work that encourages leaders to hire those with autism for those with highly developed and unique technical skills (SAP, 2019). The Autism at Work program launched in 2013 beginning with six employees with autism as system testers (SAP, 2019). The program is available in 12 countries with more than 140 autistic adults hired (SAP, 2019). The program idea began with a request for help to develop educational software for autistic children from the Autism Society of India (Florentine, 2015). The employees of the project became concerned about what type of work these children would find once adults (Florentine, 2015).

The employees learned companies do not provide a work environment that is comfortable for an autistic adult or could use autistic people's unique skills (Florentine, 2015). The employees decided to continue to work with the Autism Society on a volunteer basis to develop a program that would create a friendly work environment (Florentine, 2015). The program results identified several areas of improvement throughout the company, such as team cohesion, increase productivity and innovation, and better customer relations (Florentine, 2015).

EY, formally known as Ernst & Young, began hiring autistic adults in its Philadelphia location in 2016 (EY Global, 2018). The job, title account support associates, provides tasks to process, analyze, and organize data from several departments into one database to improve client service information (EY Global, 2018). Initial interviews conducted by phone and Skype ease the autistic workers' communication hurdles with an interview process (EY Global, 2018). After the candidate passes the initial interview, the interviewee attends a group exercise to demonstrate problem-solving skills (EY Global, 2018).

Microsoft partnered with Specialisterne, a Danish staffing organization, to develop a program to hire and assist autistic workers (Microsoft, 2019). The focus was to create an interview process with questions tailored to autistic adults and what skills would fit the company's employment needs (Microsoft, 2019). The interview process could last one week and consists of questions and workshops that allow the interviewee to demonstrate his or her unique skills in a comfortable work environment setting (Microsoft, 2019). Company leaders believe autistic workers will bring a different set of skills that will improve company performance and products (Microsoft, 2019).

In 2012, Freddie Mac partnered with Autism Self Advocacy Network (ASAN), creating an autism internship program (Freddie Mac, 2019). Freddie Mac leaders recognize the benefit of hiring autistic workers (Freddie Mac, 2019). The design of the internship program is matches autistic adults with work needs and trained managers who can assist them find a permanent position in the company (Freddie Mac, 2019). Leaders recognize each autistic individual has different skills; therefore, explore different work tasks to find a perfect position (Freddie Mac, 2019). The company has hired nine autistic adults into full-time positions of 17 interns (Freddie Mac, 2019). As suggested by Brooke et al. (2018) and Wadsworth et al. (2016), specialized designed programs for the autistic worker does help the individual adjust to the work environment and proceed to a successful career.

Discussion

The Post-Millennial generation consists of individuals who understand technology, technical devices, and social media; each a common means for digital communication (Beck & Wright, 2019; Fratricova & Kirchmayer, 2018). The number of children diagnosed with ASD continues to increase (CDC and Prevention, 2018); therefore, many Post-Millennials could have autism. Autistic children use tablets with specially designed learning software to help with developing communication and social skills, interaction with others, and speech difficulties (Autism Speaks, 2019a; Ostrow, 2014). Growing up with smart phones, tables, and computers (Seemiller & Gracem 2017), the Post-Millennial's preferred career choices are in STEM (Beck & Wright, 2019). Autistic Post-Millennials excel in technical abilities (Autism Speaks, 2019a; Beck & Wright, 2019; Ostrow, 2014; Seemiller & Gracem 2017); therefore, jobs in technology or math can prove beneficial.

Children with autism have many challenges, but they also have strengths. A variety of strengths include independent thinking, loyalty, nonjudgmental listing, understanding rules and sequences, logical thinking, decisions making, skills in math, computer, music, and art, long-term memory skills, honesty, punctuality, and visual thinkers (Sabapathy et al., 2017).

A variety of company leaders developed a safe and productive work environment for the Post-Millennial's autistic workers. Companies, such as SAP (Florentine, 2015; SAP, 2019), EY (Ernst & Young) (EY Global, 2018), Microsoft (Microsoft, 2019), and Freddie Mac (Freddie Mac, 2019, developed specialized programs to help the autistic adults find jobs and adjust to the organization's environment. Different strategies proven successful include a specialized interviewing process (EY Global, 2018; Freddie Mac, 2019; Microsoft, 2018), begin with an internship program (Freddie Mac, 2019), and match each individual to work tasks that meet their skillset (EY Global, 2018; Freddie Mac, 2019; Microsoft, 2019; SAP, 2019). EY's (EY Global, 2018), Microsoft's (2019), and SAP's (2019) leaders recognize Post-Millennial's autistic workers excel in technical skills; therefore, focus on positions that include processing information, mathematical, logical, analytical, and/or detailed.

Conclusion

Companies benefit from a diversified staff that includes people with disabilities such as ASD. A diverse workforce represents the consumer. Many companies have proven autistic employees' skills and knowledge can contribute to the company's success. The transfer from high school and/or college can be challenging for the Post-Millennial autistic adult; however, programs customized to the hiring, training, and employment of the autistic worker can help the individual adapt to a work environment. The refractive thinker considers these programs as successful business strategies for the company and the Post-Millennial autistic adult. Companies leaders from SAP, EY, Microsoft, and Freddie Mac, proved the Post-Millennial autistic adult does possess the talent for a successful career and the ability to care for themselves.

THOUGHTS FROM THE ACADEMIC ENTREPRENEUR

The problem to be solved:

- What strategies are available and successful to place Post-Millennial's autistic workers in the workforce.

The goals:

- Understanding the strategies, company leaders can implement to create a diverse workforce and safe work environment for the Post-Millennial's autistic worker.

- Presenting existing programs of strategies successfully used by well-known companies: EY, Freddie Mac, Microsoft, and SAP.

The questions to ask:

- What strategies for hiring, training, and employing Post-Millennial's autistic adults will provide a job that meets their unique skills and company goals?

- What type of program will meet the skills of the Post-Millennial autistic adult and the company goals?

Today's Business Application:

- A specialized program for hiring, training and employing the Post-Millennial's autistic adult can provide jobs to the autistic worker.

- Hiring Post-Millennial's autistic workers creates a diverse workforce that meet the company goals and represents the consumer.

REFERENCES

747 Insights. (2017). *Generation nation study*. Retrieved from https://www.747insights.com

A post millennial generation. (2018). *Phi Delta Kappan, 99*(8), 7. Retrieved from http://kappanonline.org

Autism Society. (2016a). *Facts and statistics*. Retrieved from http://www.autism-society.org/what-is/facts-and-statistics

Autism Society. (2016b). *What is autism?* Retrieved from http://www.autism-society.org

Autism Speaks Inc. (2019a). *Facts and figures*. Retrieved from https://www.autismspeaks.org/autism-facts-and-figures

Autism Speaks Inc. (2019b). *What is autism?* Retrieved from https://www.autismspeaks.org/what-autism

Beck, L., & Wright, A. (2018). iGen: What you should know about Post-Millennial students. *College and University, 94*(1), 21-26. Retrieved from https://www.aacrao.org

Brooke, V., Brooke, A. M., Schall, C., Wehman, P., McDonough, J., Thompson, K., & Smith, J. (2018). Employees with autism spectrum disorder achieving long-term employment success: A retrospective review of employment retention and intervention. *Research and Practice for Persons with Severe Disabilities, 43*(3), 181-193. doi:10.1177/1540796918783203

Bureau of Labor Statistics. (2019). Economic news release. Retrieved from https://www.bls.gov/bls/newsrels.htm#OEUS

Center for Disease Control and Prevention (CDC). (2018). *Autism spectrum disorder (ASD)*. Retrieved from https://www.cdc.gov/ncbddd/autism/data.html

EY Global. (2018). *Do great minds always think alike?* Retrieved from https://www.ey.com/en_gl/workforce/do-great-minds-always-think-alike

Florentine, S. (2015). *How SAP is hiring autistic adults for tech jobs*. Retrieved from http://www.cio.com

Fratricova, J., & Kirchmayer, Z. (2018). Barriers to work motivation of Generation Z. *Journal of Human Resource Management, 21*(2), 28-39. Retrieved from http://www.jhrm.eu

Freddie Mac. (2019). *Autism as an asset in the workplace*. Retrieved from http://www.freddiemac.com/about/people/autism-as-asset.html

Lorenz, T. Frischling, C., Cuadros, R., & Heinitz, K. (2016). Autism and overcoming job barriers: comparing job-related barriers and possible solutions in and outside of autism-specific employment. *PloS One, 11*(1), 1-19. doi:10.1371/journal.pone/0147040

McLaren, J., Lichtenstein, J. D., Lynch, D., Becker, D., & Drake, R. (2017). Individual placement and support for people with autism spectrum disorders: A pilot program. *Administration and Policy in Mental Health, 44*, 365-373. doi:10:1007/s10488-017-0792-3

Microsoft. (2019). *Global diversity and inclusion*. Retrieved from https://www.microsoft.com/en-us/diversity/inside-microsoft/cross-disability/hiring.aspx#coreui-heading-sp7tqqo

Nicholas, D. B., Mitchell, W., Dudley, C., Clarke, M., & Zulla, R. (2018). An ecosystem approach to employment and autism spectrum disorder. *Journal of Autism and Development Disorders, 48*(1), 264-275. doi:10.1007/s10803-017-3351-6

Ostrow, N. (2014). *Autism costs more than $2 million over patient's life*. Bloomberg. Retrieved from https://www.bloomberg.com/news/articles/2014-06-09/autism-costs-more-than-2-million-over-patient-s-life

Pew Research Center. (2018a). *Mobile fact sheet*. Retrieved from http://www.pew-internet.org/fact-sheet/mobile

Pew Research Center. (2018b). *The generations defined*. Retrieved from http://www.pewresearch.org/fact-tank/2018/04/11/millennials-largest-generation-us-labor-force/ft_18-04-02_generationsdefined2017_working-age/

Pew Research Center. (2018c). *U.S. labor force by generation, 1995–2015*. Retrieved from http://www.pewresearch.org/fact-tank/2018/04/11/millennials-largest-generation-us-labor-force/ft_15-05-04_genlaborforcecomposition-2/

Sabapathy, T., Madduri, N., Deavenport-Saman, A., Zamora, I., Schrager, S., & Vanderbilt, D. (2017). Parent-reported strengths in children with autism spectrum disorders at the time of an interdisciplinary diagnostic evaluation. *Journal of Developmental and Behavioral Pediatrics, 38*(3), 181-186. Retrieved from http://www.jdbp.org

Seemiller, C., & Grace, M. (2017). Generation Z: Education and engaging the next generation of students. *About Campus, 22*(3), 21-26. doi:10.1002/abc.21293

Sosnowy, C., Silverman, C., & Shattuck, P. (2018). Parents' and young adults' perspectives on transition outcomes for young adults with autism. *Autism, 22*(1), 29-39. doi:10.1177/1362361317699585

Wadsworth, S., Nelson, A., Rossi, K. D., & Hill, D. A. (2016). Connections: Parent feedback to improve social skills training for persons with autism spectrum disorder. *Journal of Applied Rehabilitations Counseling, 47*(4), 20-27. Retrieved from http://www.nationalrehabcouncelingassociation.org

Wong, P. S., Donelly, M., Neck, P. A., Boyd, B. (2018). Positive autism: Investigation of workplace characteristics leading to a strengths-based approach to employment of people with autism. *Revista de Management Comparat International, 19*(1), 15-30. doi:10.24818/RMCI.2018.1.15

About the Author...

Dr. Natalie Casale resides in Little Silver, New Jersey. Dr. Natalie holds several accredited degrees: a Bachelor of Science (BS) in Information Technology from Kean University, a Master of Business Administration (MBA) in Accounting from Monmouth University, and a Doctorate of Management (DM) in Organizational Leadership from the University of Phoenix School of Advanced Studies. Dr. Natalie is a fulltime university professor and associate online chair with Berkeley College, and part-time faculty with the University of Phoenix and Walden University. Dr. Natalie serves as a dissertation mentor / chair and committee member.

Dr. Natalie is a member of the University of Phoenix Lambda Sigma Chapter of the International Business Honor Society, Delta Mu Delta (DMD). Dr. Natalie is a volunteer National and New Jersey State District Leader of the Humane Society of the United States (HSUS) and recognized community leaders in animal welfare.

To reach Dr. Natalie Casale, please visit her **website:** http://www.nataliecasale.com or **e-mail:** nataliecasale@mac.com

CHAPTER 3

Factors Affecting Millennials' Healthcare Employees Turnover

Dr. Frank Musmar

Organizational psychologists and researchers conducted hundreds of studies on employee turnover since 1900 (Kumar & Govindarajo, 2018), because employees are an essential part of every organization regardless the size and nature of business (Low, Ong, & Tan, 2017). Despite the extensive research on employee turnover, human resource (HR) professionals struggle to retain employees (Edet, Benson, & Williams, 2017). Job embeddedness "the combined forces that keep a person from leaving his or her job" (Birsel, Boru, Islamoglu, & Yurtkoru, 2012, p. 159) became an essential goal of human resource management (HRM) practices. Justifiably, retaining talent is vital to managers in all types of organizations (Bryant & Allen, 2013).

Business leaders attempt to solve the problem differently. While some business leaders recognize the importance of managing turnover through strategies backed by research evidence, many business leaders use gut instinct (Bryant & Allen, 2013). Recognizing the complexity of the issue makes leaders' tasks of reducing employee turnover a challenge (Kim & Choi, 2015). In this chapter of the Refractive Thinker®, the author presents an overview of the relationship between job embeddedness and young healthcare employees' intention to stay with the organization. Using a refractive thinking approach, healthcare HR professionals might identify the correlation between job embeddedness and Millennials healthcare employees' intention to stay with the organization.

Background: History and Importance of Understanding Employee Turnover

Employees' decision to stay or leave an organization is a crucial variable for work-related research in all sectors of professional activity (Ferreira, Martinez, Lamelas, & Rodrigues, 2017). To understand the nature of employee turnover, it is necessary to define the terminology (Sexton, Shannon, Michalopoulos, & Smith, 2005). Whereas many definitions exist of employee turnover, turnover does not have a single, clear-cut definition (Toren, Zelker, Lipschuetz, Reicher, & Nirel, 2012). Job turnover is the rotation of staff through various labor markets and organizations as well as through different states of employment and unemployment (Aytac, Dursun, & Akalp, 2016). Poku, Behkami, and Bates (2017) defined turnover as the change by an individual from one job setting to another within the same profession. Laschinge, Read, and Zhu (2016) described turnover as withdrawal behaviors secondary to conditions within the work environment. These conditions include an increase in workloads and role ambiguity, with the association to organizational climate fostered by administration and management. Understanding the terminology of turnover is crucial to determine the factors affecting Millennials' healthcare employees' retention and to minimize the cost of turnover.

Understanding the definition of turnover is essential to the importance to differentiate between actual turnover and turnover intention. Actual turnover is the separation from the employer (Jehanzeb et al., 2013). The turnover intention is the probability that an employee will choose to leave an organization identified by specific times (Chao, Jou, Liao, & Kuo, 2015). Turnover intention is a conscious psychological willingness to leave an organization (Panatik et al., 2012) and it is "the last in a sequence of withdrawal cognitions, a set to which thinking of quitting and intent to search for alternative employment" (Tett & Meyer, 1993, p. 27).

Mobley, Griffeth, Hand, and Meglino (1979) noted that intention to quit a job is one of the strongest determinants and an immediate predecessor of turnover. Literature neglected turnover intention despite the importance of the subject (Abd-El-Salam, Shawky, & El-Nahas, 2013). The importance of differentiating between actual turnover and turnover intention will lead researchers to give more attention to turnover intention as a precaution to minimize the actual turnover.

Employee turnover is an extensively researched issue of an organizational psychologist, and collectively researchers have conducted hundreds of studies on employee turnover since 1900 (Kumar & Govindarajo, 2017). Employee turnover is an ongoing topic of research, especially in the area of public service, healthcare, hospitality, and technology sectors (Abd-El-Salam et al., 2013). Given current and ongoing predictions of nursing shortages worldwide and because the cost to organizations of both early and late turnover from the profession is high (Yang, Lv, Zhou, Liu, & Mi, 2017), turnover continues to gain increasing attention. In the United States, the demand for registered nurses (RNs) rises by 2-3% yearly, and that by the year 2025, there will be a shortage of 500,000 RNs (Yang et al., 2017). According to Yang et al. (2017), the most known cause for nursing shortage is the attrition from nurses leaving the profession. Knowing the factors affecting Millennials nurses' turnover might help (HR) to promote job embeddedness to save the cost associated with turnover

Reducing employee turnover is of high priority for leaders of every industry across the nation because of the burdensome costs associated with it (North, Rasmussen, Hughes, & Finlayson, 2005). Healthcare organizations register huge financial loses because of turnover. The cost of turnover includes not only recruitment and training costs, but also hidden costs such as productivity losses from using novice and contract registered nurses (Duffield, Roche, Homer, Buchan, & Dimitrelis, 2014). In addition, a high turnover level in the nursing field influences the turnover intention of remaining nurses, can lead to lower quality of nursing care, and cause an increase of work-related stress from excessive workloads (Duffield et al., 2014). The focus of this study was to explore the factors affecting the retention of Millennials healthcare employees in nursing homes. Failure to retain health care employees in nursing homes contributes to the poor health status of rural communities through the inability to deliver reliable and consistent services (Daufanamae, Franklin, Eagers, & Eagers, 2016). Addressing the imbalance between incentive to leave and incentive to stay might improve employee retention (Daufanamae et al., 2016).

Various strategies compacted turnover and retention within the field of nursing to address the global nursing shortage. Many RNs will leave the profession of nursing to take non-nursing positions that typically offer higher salaries, better working conditions, and better working hours (Jooste, Ehlers, & Oosthuizen, 2005). Facing the rural practice challenges are reasons for healthcare professionals to leave (Daufanamae et al., 2016). Job dissatisfaction is a significant factor in influencing healthcare employees' intention to leave their profession (Goh & Lopez, 2016). The lifestyle factors and the rural background influence the recruitment of health professionals in rural and remote communities (Edet et al., 2017). Availability of leisure and recreation activities, the proximity to the family of origin, need for healthcare employees and influence of spouse frequently contributed to recruitment decisions and retention decisions in rural areas (Edet et al., 2017). In this study, the author considered the lifestyle factors as one of the variables while studying job embeddedness of Millennials' healthcare employees in rural areas.

Nurses make up a significant proportion of the healthcare workforce (Australian Institute of Health & Welfare 2012), and their loss as a resource has implications for costs and efficiency. Nursing shortages have been a universally growing concern (Duffield et al., 2014). High employee turnover is costly and disruptive (Bryant & Allen, 2013). An organization may lose millions of dollars when an employee leaves the company, especially with the loss of a skilled employee and one in a leadership position (Amankwaa & Anku-Tsede, 2015). Employee turnover costs U.S. companies billions each year not only in direct replacement costs but also in lost productivity. High turnover affects organizational financial performance through five major cost categories: pre-departure, recruitment, selection, orientation, and lost productivity (Bryant & Allen, 2013). Health care organizations lost an estimated $1.4 to $2.1 billion each year because of RN turnover and the need to replace nurses who quit the profession (Ruiz et al., 2016). The loss of a skilled employee can be especially costly as that can lead to poor customer satisfaction ratings (Amankwaa & Anku-Tsede, 2015). Understanding the factors behind turnover might lead to Millennials' healthcare employees' job embeddedness.

Functional and Dysfunctional Turnover

Employee turnover can occur through dismissals, downsizing, and voluntary departure from an organization (Holtom & Burch, 2016). The employee turnover type most concerning to businesses is that of voluntary departure since these employees leave of their own free will and outside of the direct control of organizational leaders (Holtom & Burch, 2016). Voluntary separations are the most problematic for companies because the employee controls the separation, and often the company's investment in the employee is being lost to one of its competitors (Sexton et al., 2005).

Voluntary turnover is an inherent part of running a business, and employee turnover, in general, is a concern for any organization due to the significant impact it has on the bottom line (Low et al., 2017). Although researchers recognize the negative consequences of turnover, not all turnovers are a problem. Some scholars acknowledged the positive side of turnover or perhaps the benefits resulting from it. Some employees are not a cultural fit, do not have the skill set to perform the work, or are not motivated to work (Ahmed & Kolachi, 2013). Other professionals associated with employee turnover include getting rid of employees who are less competent and maintaining a right balance of older, more experienced employees and new employees that may bring new and fresh ideas to the organization (Edet et al., 2017), all of which can lead to improved organizational performance. The target of this study is to retain Millennials' healthcare employees that can fit professionally in the organization and can bring fresh ideas to the organization.

Mbemba, Gagnon, and Hamelin-Brabant (2016) classified employee turnover into functional and dysfunctional categories. Functional turnover occurs when poor performers leave, and good performers stay. Functional turnover occurs when the organization terminates the employment relationship. Organizations experience dysfunctional turnover when good performers' leave, and poor performers stay. Therefore, the impact on the organization–whether positive or negative–depends on the type of turnover experienced (Low et al., 2017). When looking to reduce turnover, a company focuses on dysfunctional turnover because of its negative impact on the organization.

Managing high employee turnover is critical for any organization in order to stay competitive (Anvari, Zhou JianFu, & Chermahini, 2014). Of the two types of turnover–voluntary and involuntary-the employee turnover type most concerning to businesses is that of voluntary departure because leave at their own will and their decision is beyond business leaders' control (Holtom & Burch, 2016). While acquiring and developing employees is imperative, keeping individuals have become some of the most important goals of human resource management practices (Anvari, Zhou JianFu, & Chermahini, 2014).

Employee Retention in Healthcare

Despite some studies exploring job satisfaction and different sources affecting recruitment and retention, there is a paucity of literature assessing the effectiveness of strategies to attract and retain a workforce in rural healthcare sectors (Mbemba et al., 2016). The age, demographic, professional, environmental, psychological, social and organizational factors determine the retention of health professionals (Mbemba et al., 2016). Wilson (2016) indicated that Millennials' healthcare professionals are relatively difficult to retain. Employers who wish to enhance retention of Millennials' healthcare employees need to consider the following factors: compensation and benefits, work environment, employment conditions, the opportunity for growth, and the work itself (Zhang & Fang, 2016).

There are on-going challenges in the recruitment and retention of healthcare professionals in the United States, United Kingdom (UK), Australia, Canada, and New Zealand (Uthaman, Chua, & Ang, 2016). Implementing effective recruitment and retention strategies is crucial for a successful and productive organization. Wilson (2016) stressed the importance of effective recruiting for organizations to be successful and effective recruiting included appealing to the emotions and motivations of employees. According to Wilson, recruitment will not diminish shortages without retention. Even though the literature paid a great deal of attention to employees' job mobility since the mass layoffs of the 1970s, the question of "Why do people stay in their organizations and occupations even when other opportunities are available elsewhere?" emerged as an alternative question over the past several decades (Feldeman & Ng, 2007). The shift from viewing the factors affecting turnover to the reasons for staying in the organization was the main reason for shifting toward job embeddedness. Studying the psychology of staying at a place of employment is essential to understand the factors affecting Millennials' healthcare employee's turnover.

Job Embeddedness

The psychology of staying at a place of employment is different from the psychology of leaving a place of employment, in that deciding to leave means departing from a state of familiarity (Woo & Allen, 2014). Job embeddedness is defined as "the combined forces that keep a person from leaving his or her job" (Birsel, Boru, Islamoglu, & Yurtkoru, 2012, p. 159). Woo and Allen (2014) conceptualized job embeddedness as including one's links to other aspects of the job (people and groups), perceptions of person-job fit, and sacrifices involved in leaving the job. The links aspect of embeddedness suggests that employees have formal and informal connections with other entities on the job and, as the number of those links increases, embeddedness is higher (Holtom, Mitchell, & Lee, 2006). Fit refers to the match between an employee's goals and values and those of the organization; higher fit indicates higher embeddedness (Holtom et al., 2006). Finally, sacrifice concerns the perceived costs of leaving the organization, both financial and social. The higher the perceived costs, the numerous the embeddedness occurs (Holtom et al., 2006).

The psychology of staying at a place of employment is different from the psychology of leaving a place of employment, in that deciding to leave means departing from a state of familiarity (Woo & Allen, 2014). Job embeddedness represents a different perspective in their query, and the focus is on what causes people to stay employed with a company (Ferreira et al., 2017). Business leaders have and continue to make efforts to create and expand job embeddedness in their employees to increase retention and reduce costs associated with turnover and subsequent employee training or recruitment (Ferreira et al., 2017). Sociologists have long viewed job embeddedness as an explanation of the process by which social relations influence and constrain economic action (Uzzi, 1997). Based on the sociological perspective, job embeddedness is limiting, restricting, or constraining an employee's ability to change or alter their current job situation. Alternatively, job embeddedness may not necessarily be a good thing. While job embeddedness may result in reduced turnover, it may hurt the organization's bottom line. Reduced turnover could be the case in which job embeddedness create obstacles for employees who desire to leave their current job but are restrained from doing so for various reasons, including having skills that are not transferable or inability to obtain the same benefits at another organization. Creating such obstacles could lead to an increase in workplace deviance (Ng & Feldman, 2010).

Nevertheless, interest in occupational embeddedness is increased among careers researchers (Wilson, 2016). Understanding employee embeddedness is essential for some reasons. Occupational embeddedness can explain job turnover beyond immediate situational factors (Steel, 2004). In addition, employee embeddedness is relevant to making staffing decisions. Finally, the degree of employee and embeddedness can affect the transfer of knowledge across organizational boundaries (Woo & Allen, 2014).

The Purpose of the Study

The purpose of this study was to examine the relationship between job embeddedness and Millennials healthcare employees' intention to stay with the organization. Job embeddedness is the factors that influence employee's retention. Mitchell and colleagues introduced job embeddedness in 2001. Mitchell et al. (2001) defined the job embeddedness as the on the job and off the job factors associated with individual links, fit, and sacrifice. Job embeddedness refers to examine an employee links to other people, perceptions of their fit with the job, and beliefs about what they would have to sacrifice if they left their jobs (Mitchell et al., 2001, pp. 8-9). The researcher used data from healthcare employees in the present study and used responses from participants to assess their perception of job embeddedness and work intent.

Theoretical Framework

Much of current research on voluntary turnover is grounded in March and Simon's (1958) general model of voluntary turnover, which proposes the prediction of that turnover by the perceived desirability and perceived ease of leaving an organization. Usually, job satisfaction and affective commitment capture perceived desirability, whereas perceived job alternatives represent perceived ease (Mobley, 1977; Steers & Mowday, 1981). Using field theory (Lewin, 1951), Mitchell, Lee, and colleagues (Felps et al., 2009; Mitchell et al., 2001) suggested that people may become *stuck* in their jobs and that community factors might contribute to this feeling. The authors stated that both organizational and community-related forces might prevent employees from leaving their jobs and proposed a new construct, job embeddedness, which is "like a net or a web in which an individual can become stuck" (Mitchell et al., 2001, p. 12). Mitchell et al. (2001) proposed several ways related to both on- and off-the-job factors that could embed a person in a job. Predicting *Millennials* desirability to voluntary leaving healthcare organization might help HR professionals to apply effective management strategies to prevent turnover.

The theory that served as the theoretical framework for this study is the job embeddedness theory. Mitchell, Holtom, Lee, Sablynski, and Erez (2001) developed and used job embeddedness to explain the reasons people remain at their jobs (as cited in Özçelik & Cenkci, 2014). Subsequently, Robinson, Kralj, Solnet, Goh, and Callan (2014) expanded upon the theory to explain what causes individuals to remain at their present job (as cited in Holtom & Burch, 2016). Researchers' focus on job embeddedness, because job embeddedness relates to employee turnover, increases understanding of turnover beyond employee satisfaction and commitment theory models (Basbacas & Kulik, 2013). Understanding Millennials' reasons to stay or to leave the job might help healthcare leaders to reduce the occurrences of turnover.

The key constructs of the job embeddedness theory are (a) link, (b) fit, and (c) sacrifice, with a focus on the reasons people stay with a current employer, and for potentially reducing employee turnover (Bambacas & Kulik, 2013). *Links* are either formal or informal connections between the employee and the organization (Bambacas & Kulik, 2013). *Fit* is the employee's perceived compatibility or comfort with an organization and with his or her environment (Bambacas & Kulik, 2013). Finally, *sacrifice* is the perceived financial or psychological benefits that an employee would lose when leaving current employer (Bambacas & Kulik, 2013). Researchers assess job embeddedness as a construct to account for predicting work outcomes including turnover and retention (Kiazad et al., 2015). Job embeddedness theory (Mitchell et al., 2001), an innovative and emerging research construct is a potential method of discovering the reasons people stay in an organization.

Research Questions

In the present study, I examined the following research questions:

RQ1. What is the correlation between job embeddedness and Millennials' healthcare employees' intention to stay with the organization?

RQ2. How well can job embeddedness predict Millennials' healthcare employees' intention to stay with the organization?

RQ3. What is the correlation between job link, fit, and sacrifice and Millennials' healthcare employees' intention to stay with the organization?

Method

The research design used in this study was quantitative, non-experimental, and cross-sectional design because variables of interest (work intent and job embeddedness) are naturally existing attributes. The two dimensions of the nonexperimental studies are one based on the purpose of the study (examining the relationship between job embeddedness and Millennials' healthcare employees' intention to stay with the organization) and the other on the period of the data collection (Nelson, 2017). I used a convenience sampling method and performed both multiple regression analysis as well as ANOVA. A questionnaire was used for collecting demographic data. To assess job embeddedness, I used the Job embeddedness scale (JES). To assess employees work intention, the study used the work intention inventory, short form (WII-SF).

To answer the first research question, I conducted a correlational analysis to establish if a correlation exists between the dependent (work intent) and the independent (job embeddedness) variables. To answer the second research question, I conducted a bivariate regression analysis to see how well work intent (WI) could be predicted form job embeddedness. The assessment of job embeddedness was based on the data collected through the 3 scales in the JES, namely, *fit, links,* and *sacrifice.* The assessment of intention to stay with the organization was based on the data collected through the five scales in the WII, namely employee's intent to use discretionary effort, intent to perform, intent to endorse, intent to stay, and intent to be an organization citizen.

Participants and Instrumentation

Participants in this study were 42 Millennials employees with ages between 25 and 35 years old from a rural healthcare facility in the state of Texas. The Musmar (2016) study used two instruments to collect the data for this study. The twenty-three items were taken from the Mitchell et al. (2001) organizational job embeddedness scale and used to measure organizational job embeddedness. The three scales are links, fit, and sacrifice. Sample items include "I feel like I am a good match for this company." and "I fit with the company's culture." Coefficient alpha for this scale in the study was 0.89. The Zigarmi, Nimon, Houson, Witt, and Diehl (2012) WII-SF assessed employee's intention to stay with the organization. The five scales in the WII-SF include employee's intent to use discretionary effort, intent to perform, intent to endorse, intent to stay, and intent to be an organization citizen.

Results

The data analysis indicated that there was a negative correlation between job embeddedness and work intent r (41) = -0.226, $p.$ < .01. The regression equation for predicting employees' intent to stay with the organization (WI) from job embeddedness (JE) was found to be Y' = 86.214 + -0.070 x X. The $r2$ for this equation was 0.051; that is 5.1% of the variance in WI was predictable from JE. This is a weak relationship; Even though the increase in WI tends to be associated with JE, the relationship is weak. The 95% CI for the slope to predict WI from JE ranged from 78.07 to 94.36; thus, for every unit of increase in JE, the predicted WI increased by about 78.07 to 94.36.

Assessment of the correlations between the intent to use discretionary effort, intent to perform, intent to endorse, intent to stay, intent to be an organization citizen and employees' perception of *link, fit,* and *sacrifice* were also conducted. The data analysis revealed a significant correlation between (a) job embeddedness (JE) and intent to use discretionary effort (IDE), $r(41)$ = −.318, p < .05; (b) job embeddedness (JE) and intent to stay (IS), $r(41)$ = −.433, p < .05; (c) fit and intent to stay (IS), $r(41)$ = −.469 p < .01;

(d) sacrifice (S) and intent to use discretionary effort (IDE), $r(41)$ = $-.431$, $p < .01$; (e) sacrifice and intent to perform (IP), $r(41)$ = $-.405$, $p < .01$; (f) sacrifice and intent to stay (IS), $r(41) = -.364$, $p < .05$.

Mobley et al. (1979) noted that intention to quit a job is one of the strongest determinants and an immediate predecessor of turn-over. Turnover intention is an essential issue for any organization. Surprisingly, however, there is negligence in turnover intention in the literature (Abd-El-Salam et al., 2013). For this study, I con-ducted a correlational study to explore the relationship between employee job embeddedness and their work intention. The data analysis revealed a correlation between job embeddedness and work intention, and that job embeddedness can predict work intention. Green and Salkind (2017) correlation coefficients of that 0.10, 0.30, and 0.50, irrespective of sign, or by convention, inter-preted as small, medium, and large coefficients, respectively. Job embeddedness is a comparatively new construct, and it was first introduced in 2001 (Reitz & Anderson, 2011).

The data analysis also indicated that *job embeddedness* cor-related with both *intent to use discretionary effort* and *intent to stay*. In other words, those who felt more embedded in the work-place and the community were more likely to "expand the efforts on behalf of the organization, above and beyond the agreed-upon requirements" (Zigarmi, Nimon, Witt, Diehl, 2012, p. 29) and to stay with the organization. *Fit* was correlated with *intent to stay,* and the correlation was strong. Prior research suggests that indi-viduals with poor fit are more likely to leave an organization than employees with a good person-organization fit (Reitz & Anderson, 2011). The result from this study indicated good fit was negatively correlated with work intent. Finally, the data analysis revealed that *sacrifice* was correlated with *intent to use discretionary effort, intent to perform,* and *intent to stay*. As described earlier, sacri-fice involves the ease with which links can be broken or what an employee would have to give up by breaking free of these drinks (Reitz & Anderson, 2011). The sacrifice attribute of job embeddedness is characterized as the cost of benefits that are associated with leaving a job.

Conclusion

Healthcare organizations leaders can detect turnover, retain employees and minimize the financial loses of turnover by promoting job embeddedness which might lead to increase productivity, profitability, and organizational growth. The data analysis indicated that *job embeddedness* correlated with both *intent to use discretionary effort* and *intent to stay*. Healthcare leaders that promote embeddedness are more likely to expand the efforts of Millennials on behalf of the organization, above and beyond to promote organizational commitment, increase productivity, reduce turnover, and improve the organization financial stability. Healthcare organizations leaders need to consider and implement the above strategies as a way to decrease turnover. Implementing these strategies is less expensive than the costs associated with turnover.

Therefore, recommendations include that healthcare organizations leaders, scholars, and practitioners use the findings and recommendations of this study to gain new insight into turnover intentions because the future of healthcare organizations depends on leaders' ability to retain employees. Healthcare organizations leaders who can use a refractive thinking approach in the implementation of job embedders' strategies might bring long-term success to their organizations.

THOUGHTS FROM THE ACADEMIC ENTREPRENEUR

The problem to be solved:

- Reducing employee turnover in healthcare organizations
- Improving organizations' performance by promoting job embeddedness

The goals:

- Exploring the factors affecting the retention of Millennials healthcare employees
- Improving organizational performance for sustainability

The questions to ask:

- What is the correlation between job embeddedness and healthcare employees' intention to stay with the organization?
- How well can job embeddedness predict healthcare employees' intention to stay with the organization?
- What is the correlation between job link, fit, and sacrifice and healthcare employees' intention to stay with the organization?

Today's Business Application:

- Effective leaders, who understand job turnover and employee's intention to stay, can increase productivity and profitability, which leads to organizational growth.
- The future of healthcare organizations depends on leaders' ability to retain employees.
- Supportive leaders can increase organizational productivity and performance, which in turn promotes increased sustainability.

REFERENCES

Abd-El-Salam, E. M., Shawky, A. Y., El-Nahas, T., & Nawar, Y. S. (2013). The relationship among job satisfaction, motivation, leadership, communication, and psychological empowerment: An Egyptian case study. *SAM Advanced Management Journal*, 78(2), 33-51. Retrieved from https://www.thefreelibrary.com/The+relationship+among+job+satisfaction%2c+motivation%2c+leadership%2c...-a0338323917

Ahmed, I., & Kolachi, N. A. (2013). Employee payroll and training budget: Case study of a non-teaching healthcare organization. *Journal of Business & Economics Research (Online)*, 11(5), 229. doi:10.19030/jber.v11i5.7838

Amankwaa, A., & Anku-Tsede, O. (2015). Linking transformational leadership to employee turnover: The moderating role of alternative job opportunity. *International Journal of Business Administration*, 6(4), 19. doi:10.5430/ijba.v6n4p19

Anvari, R., JianFu, Z., & Chermahini, S. H. (2014). Effective strategy for solving voluntary turnover problem among employees. *Procedia-Social and Behavioral Sciences*, 129, 186-190. doi:10.1016/j.sbspro.2014.03.665

Australian Institute of Health & Welfare. (2012). *Health expenditure Australia 2010-11* (No. 47). AIHW. Retrieved from http://www.aihw.gov.au

Aytac, S., Dursun, S., & Akalp, G. (2016). Workplace violence and effects on turnover intention and job commitment: a pilot study among healthcare workers in Turkey. *European Scientific Journal ESJ*, 12(10). doi:10.19044/esj.2016.v12n10p%25p

Bambacas, M., & Kulik, T. C. (2013). Job embeddedness in China: How HR practices impact turnover intentions. *The International Journal of Human Resource Management*, 24, 1933-1952. doi:10.1080/09585192.2012.725074

Birsel, M., Börü, M. D., İslamoğlu, G., & Yurtkoru, E. S. (2012). Job embeddedness in relation with different socio demographic characteristics. *MU Journal of Institute of Social Sciences*, 10, 51-61. doi:10.1007/978-3-319-96059-3_32

Bryant, P. C., & Allen, D. G. (2013). Compensation, benefits and employee turnover: HR strategies for retaining top talent. *Compensation & Benefits Review*, 45(3), 171-175. doi:10.1177/0886368713494342

Chao, M. C., Jou, R. C., Liao, C. C., & Kuo, C. W. (2015). Workplace stress, job satisfaction, job performance, and turnover intention of health care workers in rural Taiwan. *Asia Pacific Journal of Public Health*, 27(2), NP1827-NP1836. doi:10.1177/1010539513506604

Collins, K., Jones, M. L., McDonnell, A., Read, S., Jones, R., & Cameron, A. (2000). Do new roles contribute to job satisfaction and retention of staff in nursing and professions allied to medicine? *Journal of Nursing Management*, 8(1), 3-12. Doi:10.1046/j.1365-2834.2000.00149_8_1.x

Cunha, J. M., & Miller, T. (2014). Measuring value-added in higher education: Possibilities and limitations in the use of administrative data. *Economics of Education Review, 42*, 64-77. doi:10.1016/j.econedurev.2014.06.001

Daufanamae, B. U., Franklin, R. C., Eagers, J., & Eagers, B. D. R. F. J. (2016). Unintentional injury prevention and the role of occupational therapy in the Solomon Islands: An integrative review. *Rural and Remote Health, 16*(3810). Retrieved from http://www.rrh.org.au

Duffield, C. M., Roche, M. A., Homer, C., Buchan, J., & Dimitrelis, S. (2014). A comparative review of nurse turnover rates and costs across countries.*Journal of Advanced Nursing, 70*, 2703-2712. doi:10.1111/jan.12483

Edet, A. O., Benson, U. R., & Williams, R. E. (2017). Principals' conflict resolution strategies and teachers' job effectiveness in public secondary schools in Akwa Ibom State, Nigeria. *Journal of Educational and Social Research, 7*(2), 153-158. doi:10.5901/jesr.2017.v7n2p153

Feldman, D. C., & Ng, T. W. (2007). Careers: Mobility, embeddedness, and success. *Journal of Management, 33*, 350-377. doi:10.1177/0149206307300815

Felps, W., Mitchell, T. R., Hekman, D. R., Lee, T. W., Holtom, B. C., & Harman, W. S. (2009). Turnover contagion: How coworkers' job embeddedness and job search behaviors influence quitting. *Academy of Management Journal, 52*, 545-561. doi:10.5465/amj.2009.41331075

Ferreira, A. I., Martinez, L. F., Lamelas, J. P., & Rodrigues, R. I. (2017). Mediation of job embeddedness and satisfaction in the relationship between task characteristics and turnover: A multilevel study in Portuguese hotels. *International Journal of Contemporary Hospitality Management, 29*(1), 248-267. doi:10.1108/ijchm-03-2015-0126

Ghosh, P., Rai, A., Chauhan, R., Gupta, N., & Singh, A. (2015). Exploring the moderating role of context satisfaction between job characteristics and turnover intention of employees of Indian public sector banks. *Journal of Management Development, 34*, 1019-1030. doi:10.1108/jmd-10-2014-0138

Goh, Y. S., & Lopez, V. (2016). Job satisfaction, work environment, and intention to leave among migrant nurses working in a publicly funded tertiary hospital. *Journal of Nursing Management, 24*, 893-901. doi:10.1111/jonm.12395

Herscovitch, L., & Meyer, J. P. (2002). Commitment to organizational change: Extension of a three-component model. *Journal of Applied Psychology, 87*, 474. doi:10.1037/0021-9010.87.3.474

Holtom, B. C., & Burch, T. C. (2016). A model of turnover-based disruption in customer services. *Human Resource Management Review, 26*(1), 25-36. doi:10.1016/j.hrmr.2015.09.004

Holtom, B. C., Mitchell, T. R., & Lee, T. W. (2006). Increasing human and social capital by applying job embeddedness theory. *Organizational Dynamics, 35*, 316-331. doi:10.1016/j.orgdyn.2006.08.007

Jehanzeb, K., Rasheed, A., & Rasheed, M. F. (2013). Organizational commitment and turnover intentions: Impact of employee's training in private sector of Saudi Arabia. *International Journal of Business and Management, 8*(8), 79. doi:10.5539/ijbm.v8n8p79

Jooste, K., Ehlers, V. J., & Oosthuizen, M. J. (2005). The role played by recruitment agencies in the emigration of South African nurses. *Health SA Gesondheid, 10*(3), 57-67. doi:10.4102/hsag.v10i3.201

Keane, S., Lincoln, M., Rolfe, M., & Smith, T. (2013). Retention of the rural allied health workforce in New South Wales: A comparison of public and private practitioners. *BMC Health Services Research, 13*(1). doi:10.1186/1472-6963-13-32

Kiazad, K., Holtom, B. C., Hom, P. W., & Newman, A. (2015). Job embeddedness: A multifoci theoretical extension. *Journal of Applied Psychology, 100*, 641. doi:10.1037/a0038919

Kim, M. J., & Choi, J. S. (2015). Effects of perception of the healthcare accreditation, and job stress on turnover intention in nurses. *Journal of Muscle and Joint Health, 22*(2), 87-95. doi:10.5953/jmjh.2015.22.2.87

Kumar,D., & Govindarajo, N. S. (2014). Instrument Development "Intention to Stay Instrument" (ISI). *Asian Social Science, 10*(12). doi:10.5539/ass.v10n12p149

Laschinger, H. K., Read, E., & Zhu, J. (2016). Employee empowerment and organizational commitment. *Handbook of Employee Commitment, 319*. doi:10.4337/9781784711740.00036

Lewin, K. (1951). Field theory in social science: Selected theoretical papers. *APA Psyc Net, 25*, 409-410. doi:10.1086/638467

Low, M. P., Ong, S. F., & Tan, P. M. (2017). Would internal corporate social responsibility make a difference in professional service industry employees' turnover intention?: A two-stage approach using PLS-SEM. *Global Business and Management Research, 9*(1), 24. Retrieved from http://www.gbmrjournal.com

Matei, M. C., & Abrudan, M. M. (2016). Adapting Herzberg's two factor theory to the cultural context of Romania. *Procedia-Social and Behavioral Sciences, 221*, 95-104. doi:10.1016/j.sbspro.2016.05.094

Mbemba, G. I. C., Gagnon, M. P., & Hamelin-Brabant, L. (2016). Factors influencing recruitment and retention of healthcare workers in rural and remote areas in developed and developing countries: an overview. *Journal of Public Health in Africa, 7*(2). doi:10.4081/jphia.2016.565

Mills, A., & Millsteed, J. (2002). Retention: an unresolved workforce issue affecting rural occupational therapy services. *Australian Occupational Therapy Journal, 49*(4), 170-181. doi:10.1046/j.1440-1630.2002.00293.x

Mitchell, T. R., Holtom, B. C., Lee, T. W., Sablynski, C. J., & Erez, M. (2001). Why people stay: Using job embeddedness to predict voluntary turnover. *The Academy of Management Journal, 44*, 1102–1121. doi:10.5465/3069391

Mobley, W. H. (1977). Intermediate linkages in the relationship between job satisfaction and employee turnover. *Journal of Applied Psychology, 62*(2), 237-240. doi:10.1037/0021-9010.62.2.237

Mobley, W. H., Griffeth, R. W., Hand, H. H., & Meglino, B. M. (1979). Review and conceptual analysis of the employee turnover process. *Psychological Bulletin, 86*, 493. doi:10.1037/0033-2909.86.3.493

Musmar, F. F. (2016). *Financial distress in the health care business.* College of Management and Technology (Doctoral dissertation, Walden University). Retrieved from http://www.scholarworks.waldenu.edu

Nelson, D. L. (2017). Quantitative research designs: Defining variables and their relationships with one another. *Kielhofner's Research in Occupational Therapy: Methods of Inquiry for Enhancing Practice*, 244. Retrieved from http://www.fadavis.com

North, N., Rasmussen, E., Hughes, F., Finlayson, M., Ashton, T., Campbell, T., & Tomkins, S. (2005). Turnover amongst nurses in New Zealand's district health boards: A national survey of nursing turnover and turnover costs. *New Zealand Journal of Employment Relations, 30*(1), 49. doi:10.1111/j.1365-2834.2012.01371.x

Özçelik, G., & Cenkci, T. (2014). Moderating effects of job embeddedness on the relationship between paternalistic leadership and in-role job performance. *Procedia-Social and Behavioral Sciences, 150*, 872-880. doi:10.1016/j.sbspro.2014.09.096

Panatik, S., Rajab, A., Shaari, R., Shah, I. M., Rahman, H. A., & Badri, S. Z. (2012). Impact of work-related stress on well-being among academician in Malaysian Research University. In *International conference on education and management innovation* (Vol. 30, pp. 37-41). Retrieved from http://www.ipedr.com

Peltokorpi, V. (2013). Job embeddedness in Japanese organizations. *The International Journal of Human Resource Management, 24*, 1551-1569. doi:10.1080/09 585192.2012.723636

Pittino, D., Visintin, F., Lenger, T., & Sternad, D. (2016). Are high performance work practices really necessary in family SMEs? An analysis of the impact on employee retention. *Journal of Family Business Strategy, 7*(2), 75-89. doi:10.1016/j.jfbs.2016.04.002

Poku, M. K., Behkami, N. A., & Bates, D. W. (2017). Patient relationship management: What the U.S. healthcare system can learn from other industries. *Journal of General Internal Medicine, 32*(1), 101-104. doi:10.1007/s11606-016-3836-6

Reitz, O. E., & Anderson, M. A. (2011). An overview of job embeddedness. *Journal of Professional Nursing, 27*(5), 320-327. doi:10.1016/j.profnurs.2011.04.004

Robinson, R. N., Kralj, A., Solnet, D. J., Goh, E., & Callan, V. (2014). Thinking job embeddedness not turnover: Towards a better understanding of frontline hotel worker retention. *International Journal of Hospitality Management*, *36*, 101-109. doi:10.1016/j.ijhm.2013.08.008

Ruiz, P. B. D. O., Perroca, M. G., & Jericó, M. D. C. (2016). Cost of nursing turnover in a teaching hospital. *Revista da Escola de Enfermagem da USP*, *50*(1), 101-108. doi:10.1590/s0080-623420160000100014

Sexton, R. S., McMurtrey, S., Michalopoulos, J. O., & Smith, A. M. (2005). Employee turnover: A neural network solution. *Computers & Operations Research*, *32*, 2635-2651. doi:10.1016/j.cor.2004.06.022

Solomon, P., Salvatori, P., & Berry, S. (2001). Perceptions of important retention and recruitment factors by therapists in northwestern Ontario. *The Journal of Rural Health*, *17*(3), 278-285. doi:10.1111/j.1748-0361.2001.tb00965.x

Steel, R. P. (2004). Job markets and turnover decisions. *Innovative Theory and Empirical Research on Employee Turnover*, 73-82. Retrieved from http://www.infoagepub.com

Steers, R. M., & Mowday, R. T. (1981). Employee turnover and post-decision justification. *Research in Organizational Behavior*, *3*, 235-282. Retrieved from http://apps.dtic.mil

Tett, R. P., & Meyer, J. P. (1993). Job satisfaction, organizational commitment, turnover intention, and turnover: path analyses based on meta analytic findings. *Personnel Psychology*, *46*(2), 259-293. doi:10.1111/j.1744-6570.1993.tb00874.x

Toren, O., Zelker, R., Lipschuetz, M., Riba, S., Reicher, S., & Nirel, N. (2012). Turnover of registered nurses in Israel: characteristics and predictors. *Health Policy*, *105*(2-3), 203-213. doi:10.1016/j.healthpol.2012.03.002

Uthaman, T., Chua, T. L., & Ang, S. Y. (2016). Older nurses: A literature review on challenges, factors in early retirement and workforce retention. *Proceedings of Singapore Healthcare*, *25*(1), 50-55. doi:10.1177/2010105815610138

Uzzi, B. (1997). Towards a network perspective on organizational decline. *International Journal of Sociology and Social Policy*, *17*(7/8), 111-155. doi:10.1108/s0742-3322(2013)0000030014

Vaid, D. (2012). The caste-class association in India. *Asian Survey*, *52*, 395-422. doi:10.1525/as.2012.52.2.395

Wilson, D. R. (2016). Healthcare manager's perception of how empowerment is experienced working among their employees. *Conflict Resolution & Negotiation Journal*, *2016*(2).

Woo, S. E., & Allen, D. G. (2014). Toward an inductive theory of stayers and seekers in the organization. *Journal of Business and Psychology*, *29*, 683-703. doi:10.1007/s10869-013-9303-z

Yang, H., Lv, J., Zhou, X., Liu, H., & Mi, B. (2017). Validation of work pressure and associated factors influencing hospital nurse turnover: A cross-sectional investigation in Shaanxi Province, China. *BMC Health Services Research, 17*(1), 112. doi:10.1186/s12913-017-2056-z

Yan, Y. I. N. (2015). How to use Maslow's Hierarchical theory of needs to excite the work enthusiasm of archivists. *Shanxi Science and Technology, 3,* 017. Retrieved from http://www.simplypsychology.org

Zigarmi, D., Nimon, K., Houson, D., Witt, D., & Diehl, J. (2012). The work intention inventory: Initial evidence of construct validity. *Journal of Business Administration Research, 1*(1), 24. doi:10.5430/jbar.v1n1p24

Zhang, X., & Fang, P. (2016). Job satisfaction of village doctors during the new healthcare reforms in China. *Australian Health Review, 40*(2), 225-233. doi:10.1071/ah15205

About the Author . . .

Dr. Frank Musmar resides in Texas and is currently an adjunct professor at Louisiana International College and American Management and Technology Universities. Dr. Musmar received his Doctorate of Business Administration in healthcare management from Walden University in 2016 and a Master of Science in Biotechnology Management from the University of Maryland in 2011. Dr. Musmar is the founder and the Lead Dissertations Consultant at Editors Dissertations and Thesis.

Dr. Frank is also an active member of the Delta Mu Delta Honor Society, Sigma Alpha Pi Honor Society, and Golden Key International Honor Society. Dr. Musmar is a certified Executive leader through the National Society of Leadership and Success.

He has published three journal publications: *Job Embeddedness and Employee Retention in Healthcare, Financial Distress at Nonprofit Organizations,* and *Once-Daily Oral Medication for Treatment of Cognitive Dysfunction in Down Syndrome.* Additional work includes his dissertation: *Financial Distress in the Health Care Business.*

With more than 26 years of experience in business and 8 years in higher education, I used my career and education to help my colleges and alumni to develop and advance career path. Today as Dissertation Editing and Proofreading specialist | Best Selling Writer | Faculty | Financial and Performance Management Specialist I would like to be involved in strategies to direct students and Alumni to achieve a better career and financial stability.

To reach Dr. Frank Musmar, please visit his **websites:** http://www.editors dissertationsandthesis.com or **e-mail:** frankmusmar@gmail.com

LinkedIn: https://www.linkedin.com/in/dr-frank-musmar-231b2417/ **Tel:** (469)765-6163

CHAPTER 4

Consideration of a Diverse Multigenerational Cybersecure Workforce

Dr. Avideh Sadaghiani-Tabrizi

Generations X, Y (referred to as the Millennials), and Z or the Digital Natives, working together with Baby Boomers create seismic changes in the state of organizational culture and workforce amid the new economy's digitally-advanced landscape. The Millennials and Digital Native might have different cybersecurity values and attitudes from those in generation X and Baby Boomers, unique to each generation's cybersecurity habits. Consideration to revise the cybersecurity policies and efforts, and network security and information security could help to identify and detect security-incidents, data security issues with big data, and identification of Internet activities in the event of threats of cyber-attacks in the global interconnected economy. This chapter's purpose is to introduce organizations' refractive thinking and vigilance, in addressing risks of unscrupulous threat actors to mitigate data security events, which might help to implement cyber-resiliency against the threats of attacks by adversaries. The gap in the age of Baby Boomers (1946 to 1964), generations Xers (1965 to 1979), Yers (1980 to 1994), and Zers (1995 to 2012) who could dominate the workforce, might introduce new vulnerabilities, ranging from server and virtualization sprawl vulnerabilities to breaches, brute force attacks, and data theft.

The organizations' attempt to divert procedures for sophisticated monitoring systems and flash technology might help to alleviate the effect of data breaches through consideration of implementing resilient cyber-ecosystems and acquiring liability coverage, in a digital-landscape with the basic composition of the generational makeup for organizations, which could span 40 years. The continual examination of business continuity, productivity, and restoration plans might help organizations to achieve advancements in technologies in the competitive global economy, requiring management's effective governance strategies, evaluation of organizational security postures across the workforce influx, and mitigation to deal with risks (Ciampa, 2017). Many innovations in communication systems have eased organizational interactions through collaboration, by removing barriers to sharing information that might need sustainability of organization's continuity in overcoming the threats of catastrophic cybersecurity attacks. Accordingly, the various views on technology use in the workforce might align with the differences in technology use and cohorts' stereotypes placed on generational career aspirations of a multigenerational workforce (Ostrowski, 2018). The resiliency of the cyber-ecosystem might present the demography of workplaces with investments in information security to go beyond protecting the businesses against cyber-attacks, with an approach to protect the privacy and organizational assets, strategically.

The number of attacks on organizations increase, continually directing attention to differing cybersecurity practices among the employees in multigenerational workforce. A variety of risks might necessitate consideration of several factors in the cybersecurity policies, with the Baby Boomers, generations X, Millennials, and Digital Natives' level of cyber awareness and compliance. Detection of network anomalies of behaviors, in an increasingly sophisticated and interconnected global Internet environment could be helpful, in distinguishing between an evidence for compromise of data and security incidents, in a world where data and information security is at risk, and attacks escalate (Ciampa, 2017; Raghavan, 2016). Accordingly, several security principles are fundamental to withstand attacks in addition to technological defenses, to serve as a foundation to security of systems through "layering, limiting, diversity, obscurity, and simplicity" (Ciampa, 2017, p. 32). Digital signatures, network system activity logs, definitive activity and behavior of users' records and transactions, mobile devices, evidence of compromise, identification of data, intrusion detection systems, servers, and networks could provide valuable machine data, given the rapid pace in innovations, "in the cybersecurity field" (Shackelford & Brady, 2018, p. 1). An effective and well-written cybersecurity policy, addressing the threats from a variety of behaviors and risks with the generational divide for different reasons, might provide direction to accommodate a healthy balance between work and lives of employees, and address many needs of a multi-generational workforce with differing values and expectations.

Management of a workforce with complex technology devices might involve integration of intricate and interrelated modes of communication that could lead an organization to catastrophic outcomes (Shackelford & Brady, 2018). Mitigation of a variety of cybersecurity risks, from falling prey to social engineering and phishing scams, break in security on WiFi networks, to the use of unsafe applications might be necessary to adapt to more advanced security processes, more than ever when many Baby Boomers could exit the workforce. Workplaces could employ people from all four generations: (a) Baby Boomers; (b) generation Xers; (c) generation Yers (Millennials); and (d) generation Zers (Digital Natives), with various cybersecurity habits on the Internet, leaving organization vulnerable to targeted attacks with advanced persistent threats and strategic web attacks to compromise organizational networks.

Challenges to Privacy

The loss of data could increase the risks of identity theft, using stolen electronic data through viruses, worms, Trojans, and botnets attacks to exemplify the harms, which many organizations could realize. Organizations' culture and assessment of the threat environment to address many needs, beyond standards might help to avoid data breaches, viruses, phishing attacks, worms, and botnets through implementation of organization's social responsibility, in fulfilling social functions to provide accommodations (Secureworks, 2017; Vettori, 2005). Organizations benefit from mitigation of risks of advanced persistent threats that is referred to as APTs. Mitigating strategic compromise or "watering hole attacks" (Alrwais, Yuan, Alowaisheq, Liao, Oprea, Wang, & Li, 2016, p. 1), involving zero-day exploits, leave organizations' internal networks vulnerable to infiltrate malicious software that is referred to as malware on websites, could be beneficial in mitigating a variety of Internet crimes. Threats of phishing, unsolicited emails and texts, and fraudulent phone calls and impersonation scams, which could mask the senders' identification or callers' phone number through id-spoofing that falsify the transmitted information, result from exploiting a vulnerability in the public switched telephone network could pose dangers to vulnerabilities to imperil victims.

The two categories of personnel in information security who are responsible to provide enterprise protection for organizations are; information security technical and managerial personnel, designing, configuring installations to maintain technical security equipment, and administering, managing processes, people, plans, and policies. A refractive approach to evaluate the three layers in security might help the implementation, establishing procedures and policies for people to "use the products correctly" (Ciampa, 2017, p. 20). Regulating the connected devices and computers, which connect to the Internet and risk becoming infected in seconds might help with protection of organizational assets, data and connection vulnerabilities, which threat actors could exploit (Ciampa, 2017). For example, mobile devices could risk sharing an Internet connection with "other mobile devices through Bluetooth or Wi-Fi" (Ciampa, 2017, p. 436), when tethering to open a door to vulnerability of infecting other mobile devices or corporate network. Additionally, mobile devices could connect to the network through a universal serial bus (USB) connection. Accordingly, a host device could act as a peripheral to "an external media access" [to introduce malware on the mobile device that is also known as] "USB On-the-Go (OTG)" [allowing attackers to snoop or] "eavesdrop on the data transmission" (Ciampa, 2017, p. 463).

Attackers could view confidential and sensitive information on mobile devices, which connect to public network to access the Internet and allow attackers to access content through jailbreaking, rooting, sideloading, short message service (SMS). Custom firmware could present another layer of security vulnerability for mobile devices. A variety of connections to quick response (QR) codes, which include "a matrix or two-dimensional barcode" [that was] "designed for the automotive industry in Japan," [originally. QR gained popularity outside of] "the automotive industry" [to] "store website URLs, plain text, phone numbers, email addresses," [or] "any alphanumeric data up to 4296 characters" (Ciampa, 2017, p. 464). QR consists of black modules or square dots, which are "arranged in a square grid on a white background," [and often] "read by an imaging device such as a mobile device's camera" (author, year, p. 463). Accordingly, unaware access could allow an attacker to introduce malware, other untrusted applications, and threats to a connected device to allow an attack threat vector, and to eaves drop on the vulnerable connection.

The public switched telephone network operates through voice-over-Internet-protocol (VOIP), which might require organizational policies and awareness to defend against impersonation scams who could evade the caller's identification, to open a back-door channel to an organization. The organizational resources could risk falling prey to voice phishing that is also known as vishing or vishing scams through a "growing access to the PSTN from the Internet," [and the availability of] "many internet telephone service providers (ITSPs)" (Tu, 2017, p. 23), customizing and spoofing caller IDs. Spoofing caller IDs include "circumventing call blockers," [and evading the caller's identification to defeat call blockers and defenses for a variety of anti-spam to further] "a variety of scams" (Tu, 2017, p. 4). Organizations could risk impersonation scams through a wide-variety of threats, to hide information about a threat actor, and the dissemination of telephone spams through robocalling, using an auto-dialer to dial a phone number, automatically delivering "voice or voicemail messages to a list of phone numbers" (Tu, 2017, p. 13) through voicemail-injection. The aggregation of voice-and-Internet communication with artificial intelligence programs' use of modern technologies to disguise, parse, and analyze information, direct attention to greater emphasis on monitoring of internetworking, communication, and exercise of cybersecurity awareness (Oltsik, 2018), through four methodologies: (a) anomaly, (b) signature-based, (c) behavior, and (d) heuristic monitoring. Threat actors could target vulnerabilities to utilize attacks in forms of threat vectors and find a whole in a system to spear-phish forms of hacking attempts, in targeting an attack and to gain an advantage over intellectual property (Ferrillo, 2015). Organizational data privacy and securing network centers are contrary to convenience, in avoiding the presence of malicious behavior and cybersecurity risks, and do not limit to malware and Internet frauds with the introduction of the robocalling. Organizations use of optical circuit-switching could help to provide a hybrid design in the switching technologies to channel communication, efficiently, with intrusion detection technologies to detect threats of interception and to monitor systems' information packets on a host and network to identify anomalies.

Resiliency in a Cyber-ecosystem

Various forms of malware, capable of causing threats to exploit vulnerabilities might require computer and cybersecurity awareness, diligence and literacy in developing resiliency to much of the problems, which are harmful to all generations on the Internet, in environments as such in e-mails' spam and denial of service attacks. The endless cycle of identification of vulnerabilities, risks and response plans for evaluating exposure, availability and reliability of resources, written cyber-policies, heterogeneity in roles, and effective strategies for resiliency in the cyber-ecosystems require resiliency against various forms of targeted attacks. Attackers could utilize many attack-tools to execute zero-day attacks on vulnerable networks, causing resource exhaustion in a variety of enterprises in forms of threat actors, to collecting competitive information for "political, economic, technical, or military" (Giandomenico, 2017, para. 6) gains. The digital future, big data and exponential data-growth, increases in users' expectations, and the threats of a cyber-attack could contribute, to organizations and leaders' concerns over management of data and strategies. The advancements in IT developments, communication systems, and processing information in digital forms could contribute to changes in engaging and transacting on the Internet (The Levin Institute, 2014). The increases in customer expectation might direct organizational leaders to exercise resiliency, to protect data. The implementation of National Institute of Standards (NIST) cybersecurity framework of the Organization for Standardization (ISO-27001), and to provide a holistic approach to manage risks, proactively through a set of standards for managing the core components of security.

People, processes, and technologies with an adaptive-security framework incident-response plans (IRP), business-continuity plan (BCP), and intrusion-detection system could help to improve cybersecurity programs in multigenerational organizations, avoiding malware to reduce targeted-phishing-attacks. Identification and protection of assets could be another element to detect and respond to threats in exercising resiliency to recover from a breach (Ferrillo, 2015; Homeland Security, 2018). A cyber breach identifies as a data-security event, compromising individuals' confidential and, or sensitive private and propriety information, victimizing data to unauthorized and, or bad actors. The resiliency to resist, react, and recover from threats of an attack in the cyber-ecosystem might require sustainability of organizations to leverage risks of the cultural norms, to preserve the confidentiality, integrity, and availability of organizational assets. The technology solutions, consisting of firewalls, antivirus software, and controlling user's access and management processes might require resiliency in the leadership and culture, for creating sustainable benefits over the cyber criminals and malicious actors (EY, 2014).

Cyber-resiliency of organizations might account for dangers of cyberattacks, which are abundant and lurking for recurrent threats with any new technology, or revitalization of an old technology within the ecosystem of digital world (Valdetero & Zetoony, 2014). As such, in May 2017, the WannaCry ransomware cryptoworm threat vector targeted and spread to encrypt over 200,000 computers, worldwide in over 150 nations, which made demands for bitcoin payment to free the computer and unlock the data, destabilizing privacy means (Sheedy, 2018). Accordingly, to prevent these potential effects might necessitate awareness and a good strategy to defend against attacks across all generations in today's workforce. Alignment of efforts with the Federal Trade Commission and others could serve network systems as a security resource, given the massive growth of data, to extract signatures in the event of an attack on a network, detecting intelligence to inform and perform forensics about threat vulnerabilities, actors, and vectors. Protection of the multiple layers of information and implementation of cybersecurity policies requires consideration of several factors to protect against attacks from "script kiddies, hactivists, nation state actors, insiders, and others" (Ciampa, 2017, p. 29), such as the telephony spammers who commit voice frauds. Accordingly, phone frauds occurring over the VOIP network, through "establishing a direct connection between any two points to carry analog signals modulated to voice frequencies" (Tu, 2017, p. 7), might require approaching security from multitude of layers. Security could analogize with an onion, in which multiple defenses could provide layers of security to, and against threat agents to provide protection of organizational assets.

Addressing Challenges with Security

Management of information systems of high-risk technologies might require reassessment of cybersecurity policies, in identification of threats and detection of vulnerabilities, analogizing management information systems to the nervous system, shedding light on the importance of securing confidentiality, availability, and the integrity of data in organizations, in which many adverse effects could result from the exposure and loss of data (Wawak, 2010). Establishment of a regulatory board that functions similar to the National Transportation Safety Board (NTSB) might aid organizations to investigate threats of data breach and cyberattacks as a National Cybersecurity Safety Board (NCSB) (Shackelford & Brady, 2018). Many collaborative political efforts and standards have been instrumental, in investigating risks of "the destabilizing and damaging cyberattacks," [with] "past public-private collaborations" (Shackelford & Brady, 2018, p. 1) to address risks, which each generation might present to adapt to more advanced security processes.

Consideration of many factors, in which each of the generations might lack some aspects of cybersecurity awareness could benefit from a safety board on a national level could help to mitigate the risk of a threat from the destabilizing cybersecurity world. The establishment of NCSB might help the globalization efforts, in addressing the destabilizing cybersecurity issues with "the rapid pace of technical innovation in the cybersecurity field" (Shackelford & Brady, 2018, p. 1) that ties the world with the four generations of Baby Boomers, Xers, Yers, and Zers, in regulating the disruptive technologies. Attacks, relating to many cybersecurity vulnerabilities could be numerous, diverse, damaging, and disruptive to organizations, in which the availability of open-source software, collecting information to extrapolate data into concise set of statistical algorithms and analytics to make decisions, might require organizations' continual practice of monitoring Internet activities. The malware, phishing and social engineering attacks could wreak havoc on an organization's state of security, to cause vulnerabilities through exposure of Internet openings in a cyber-connected and global workforce. The nonkinetic aspect of cyberattacks in the cyberspace could target organizations beyond reach.

Emerging Threats

The diversity of ages in a multigenerational workforce could expand upon the symbiotic fruition of innovative pedagogies to add value, offsetting challenges in managing cohorts. Reevaluation of organizational policies might help to understand leveraging management of a multigenerational workforce, with differing values and experiences in technology use. High performance computing might help organization to strive achievement of comfort and avoid conflicts that would impede the effectiveness of the workforce (Zopiatis, Krambia-Kapardis, & Varnavas, 2012). The consideration of a global multigenerational workforce might introduce an emergence with worldwide consequences of Internet and media technologies, enriching the cultural experiences to transcend national boundaries and create a global, generational consciousness and shifting demographics. The workforce of the postwar generation of Baby Boomers who might retire in the upcoming years, with generations X and Y or the Millennial s, represents cultures with unique "set of expectations, demands, and work habits" (Ng, Lyons, & Schweitzer 2012). The changes in the culture and demographics of the Millennial generation whose set of values, attitudes, and expectations differ from the Baby Boomer generation and generation Xers could be recognized though the environments, which the employers could create to engage Millennials.

The organizations adapt, increasingly to the variation of cybersecure and cultural norms, attracting to retain the highest quality of employees, in which the organizational success correlates to the employees' qualities and unique perspectives, in the fast paced world of technological innovations. Additionally, the ambiguity of cyber-threats might introduce other difficulties and disruptions, in detecting the weakest links in many cyber-attacks imposed on organizations, risking possible distributed denial of service (DDoS) attacks. Zeadally and Flowers (2014) introduced the conceptual framework of insidious possible nature of cyberwar that could impose risks of threat on organization in a "cyber-connected and cyber-dependent world," [with] "kinetic and non-kinetic activities" (Zeadally & Flowers, 2014, p. 14), associating with motion and logistics, disruption, or intelligence in wars. The organization-wide cybersecurity awareness of the entire workforce could help to alleviate risks of threats from any possible forthcoming cyberattack and cyberwar, and cyberespionage and attack vectors through Botnets, DDoS, structured query language (SQL) injection, and cross-site scripting.

In conclusion, the disruptive nature of any new complex system or technology could create vulnerabilities and cybersecurity mishaps, which might be alleviated through the process and development of cybersecurity policies in multigenerational workforce environments. An organizational cybersecurity awareness and practices approach through implementation of training from various angles, to accommodate generational training preferences might help to address the security risks, which each generation might present. Therefore, cybersecurity policies need implementation of best practices addressing the different strategies, alleviating the various security risks of non-kinetic activities, complementing and aligning with the mitigation of cybersecurity risks from phishing and social-engineering scams, to neglecting security policies and unapproved application downloads (Keystone Technologies, 2018). Utilizing the National Institute for Standards and Technology Cybersecurity Framework (NIST CSF) might help to guide the multigenerational workforce, in framing cybersecurity efforts.

THOUGHTS FROM THE ACADEMIC ENTREPRENEUR

The problem to be solved:

- Provide strategic solutions for securing information technology in not-for-profit and for-profit organization to offset dollars spent on projects, cost overruns, and cancelations.
- Ineffective team leadership that influences project performance.
- Assess the new threats of modern attacks.
- Provide rapid response to technological changes, and to re-align needs to counter volatilities in disruptive nature of technologies.

The goals:

- Assess current organizational strategies to include project teams in an earlier stage of strategic planning
- Enhance team leadership skillset when managing multiple type compositions simultaneously

The questions to ask:

- How can nonprofit and for-profit businesses be augmented to improve project team's performance?
- How can evolvable strategy benefit organizational strategies for various not-for-profit and for-profit industries?

Today's Business Application:

- Assess the practically of evolvability strategy in existing organizational strategies.
- Treat team leadership as a practitioner's field and enhance skillset to accommodate managing multiple types of teams (traditional, virtual, and hybrid) concurrently.

REFERENCES

Alrwais, S., Yuan, K., Alowaisheq, E., Liao, X., Oprea, A., Wang, X., & Li, Z. (2016). *Catching predators at watering holes: Finding and understanding strategically compromised websites.* Retrieved from http://www.ccs.neu.edu/home/alina/papers/WateringHole.pdf

Australian Government-Business (2018, July). *Keep your business safe from cyber threats.* Retrieved from https://www.business.gov.au/risk-management/cyber-security/keep-your-business-safe-from-cyber-threats

Brady, C. (2010). *Security awareness for children.* Royal Holloway, University of London. Retrieved from https://www.ma.rhul.ac.uk/static/techrep/2010/RHUL-MA-2010-05.pdf

Brändström, C. (2011). *Using the Internet in education–strengths and weaknesses: A qualitative study of teachers' opinions on the use of the Internet in planning and instruction.* Crain Communications, Inc. Retrieved from http://hig.diva-portal.org/smash/get/diva2:438827/FULLTEXT01

Business Solver. (2018). *State of empathy 2018 executive summary: Strengthening business for sustainable success.* ®Businessolver.com, Inc. 2018. Retrieved from https://info.businessolver.com/hubfs/empathy-2018/businessolver-empathy-executive-summary.pdf?hsCtaTracking=7e237aa9-1d60-4cfb-b9a9-2b881143391a%7C0c012412-b9e0-488a-8f56-4c153450c4fa

Cashell, B., Jackson, W. D., Jickling, M., & Webel, B. (2004). *The economic impact of cyber-attacks. Government and Finance Division-CRS Report for Congress.* Retrieved from http://www.au.af.mil/au/awc/awcgate/crs/rl32331.pdf

Ciampa, M. (2017). *Security+ guide to network security fundamentals* (6th ed.). Washington, DC: CompTIA.

CISCO Public (2016). Cyber resilience: Safeguarding the digital organization. CISCO and, or its affiliates. Retrieved from https://www.cisco.com/c/dam/en_us/about/doing_business/trust-center/docs/cisco-cyber-resilience-safeguarding-digital-org-wp.pdf

Cybersecurity, innovation, and the internet economy. (2011, June). *The Department of Commerce Internet Policy Task Force.* Retrieved from http://www.nist.gov/itl/upload/Cybersecurity_Green-Paper_FinalVersion.pdf

Dawson, J., & Thomson, R. (2018). The future cybersecurity workforce: Going beyond technical skills for successful cyber performance. *Front. Psychol, 9*(744). doi:10.3389/fpsyg.2018.00744

Drucker, P. (1954). *The practice of management.* New York, NY: HarperCollins Publishers.

Duffy, T. (2015, October). Malware wears costumes, too. *Center for Internet Security, Monthly Security Tips Newsletter. Multi-State Information Sharing &*

Analysis Center, The Center for Internet Security (CIS): *Stop, Think, Connect Campaign Monthly Security Tips.* Retrieved from http://msisac.cisecurity.org/newsletters/2015-10.cfm

Dwyer, R. & Azevedo, A. (2016). Preparing leaders for the multi-generational workforce. *Journal of Enterprising Communities: People and Places in the Global Economy, 10*(3), 281-305. https://dx.doi-org.contentproxy.phoenix.edu/10.1108/JEC-08-2013-0025

Eddy, S., Ng, W., Schweitzer, L., & Lyons, S. (2010). New generation, great expectations: A field study of the millennial generation. *Journal of Business and Psychology, 25,* 281-292. http://dx.doi.org/10.1007/s10869-010-9159-4

EY (2014, Dec). *Achieving resilience in the cyber ecosystem: Rise of the cyber ecosystem.* EYGM Limited. Retrieved from https://www.ey.com/Publication/vwLU-Assets/cyber_ecosystem/$FILE/EY-Insights_on_GRC_Cyber_ecosystem.pdf

Ferrillo, P. A. (2015). *Navigating cybersecurity storm: A guide for directors and officers.* Advisen, Ltd. Retrieved from https://cybersummitusa.com/wp-content/uploads/2015/12/navigatingcybersecuritystorm-paulferrillo.pdf

Fidler, D. P. (2018). *Cybersecurity and the new era of space activities.* Maurer School of Law: Indiana University Digital Repository @ Maurer Law. Retrieved from https://www.repository.law.indiana.edu/cgi/viewcontent.cgi?article=3665&context=facpub

FireEye. (2018). *Anatomy of advanced persistent threats: If you know how they work, you can learn how to stop them.* Retrieved from https://www.fireeye.com/current-threats/anatomy-of-a-cyber-attack.html

Frechtling, J., & Sharp, L. (Eds.). (1997). *User-friendly handbook for mixed method evaluation.* Arlington, VA: National Science Foundation.

Friel, A. (2011). Digital media: Handle with care. *Law Technology News.* Retrieved from http://www.law.com/jsp/lawtechnologynews/PubArticleFriendlyLTN.jsp?id=1202536525505

GetSmarter (2018). *The strengths and weaknesses of every generation in your workforce.* GetSmarter | A brand of 2U, Inc. Retrieved from https://www.getsmarter.com/blog/career-advice/know-your-generationals/

Giandomenico, A. (2017). *Know your enemy: Understanding threat actors.* Retrieved from https://www.csoonline.com/article/3203804/security/know-your-enemy-understanding-threat-actors.html

Greene, J., Caracelli, V., & Graham, W. (1989). Toward a conceptual framework for mixed-method evaluation designs. *Educational Evaluation and Policy Analysis, 11*(3), 255–274. doi:10.3102/01623737011003255

Griffith, G., & Roth, L. (2007, September). *Protecting children from online sexual predators.* Retrieved from http://www.parliament.nsw.gov.au/prod/parlment/publications.nsf/0/3043e49ab3f4abf9ca25735006f989/$file/dealing%20with%20online%20predatorsfinal&index.pdf

Haghi, M., Thurow, K., Habil, I., Stoll, R., & Habil, M. (2017, January). *Wearable devices in medical Internet of things: Scientific research and commercially available devices.* Retrieved from https://synapse.koreamed.org/DOIx. php?id=10.4258/hir.2017.23.1.4

Hassanalieragh, M., Page, A., Soyata, T., Sharma, G., Aktas, M., Mateos, G., Kantarci, B., & Andreescu, S. (2015). Health monitoring and management using Internet-of-Things (IoT) sensing with cloud-based processing: Opportunities and challenges. doi:10.1109/GLOCOM.2015.7417414

Homeland Security. (2018). *Official website of the Department of Homeland Security: National cybersecurity awareness month.* Retrieved from https://www. dhs.gov/national-cyber-security-awareness-month

Horowitz, M. C., March, G., & Scharre, P. (2015). *The morality of robotic war.* New York Times Company. Retrieved from https://www.nytimes. com/2015/05/27/opinion/the-morality-of-robotic-war.html

Imran, M., Collier, M., Landais, P., & Katrinis, K. (2015). Software-controlled next generation optical circuit switching for HPC and cloud computing datacenters. *Electronics 2015, 4*, 909-921. https://dx.doi.org/10.3390/electronics4040909

Intersog. (2017, July). *How blockchain technology can take eHealth app development to the next level.* [Web log comment]. Retrieved from https://ehealth. intersog.com/blog/how-blockchain-technology-can-take-ehealth-app-development-to-the-next-level

Jiang, M., Hsin-yi, S., Tsai, S. Cotten, S.R., Rifon, N.J., LaRose, R. & Saleem Alhabash, S. (2016). *Educational Gerontology.* Rutledge Taylor & Francis Group. http://dx.doi.org/10.1080/03601277.2016.1205408

Keating, M., Wiles, J., & Wood-Piazza, M. (2002). *Learning webs: Curriculum journeys on the Internet.* Englewood Cliffs, NJ: Merrill / Prentice Hall.

Keenan, T. P. (2014). *Techno creep: The surrender of privacy and the capitalization of intimacy.* New York, NY: OR Books.

Keller, J. (2015, September 18). *Air Force reaches out to industry for ways to ensure communications in nuclear events.* Retrieved from http://www.militaryaerospace.com/articles/2015/09/nuclear-military-communications.html

Kaspersky Lab. (2018, May). *Who's who in the zoo: Cyberespionage operation targets Android users in the middle east.* Retrieved from https://media.kaspersky-contenthub.com/wp-content/uploads/sites/43/2018/05/03114450/ZooPark_for_ public_final_edit.pdf

Keystone Technologies. (2018, January). *Cybersecurity policies for a multi-generational workplace.* Retrieved from http://keystonetech.ca/2018/01/08/ cybersecurity-policies-multi-generational-workplace/

Krumm, J. (2010). *Ubiquitous computing fundamentals.* Boca Raton, FL: CRC Press.

Lewis, L. F., & Wescott, H. D. (2017). *Multi-generational workforce: Four generations united in lean. Journal of Business Studies Quarterly, 8*(3), 1-14.

Lewis, J. A. (2018, January). *Rethinking cybersecurity: Strategy, mass effect, and states.* Retrieved from https://csis-prod.s3.amazonaws.com/s3fs-public/publication/180108_Lewis_ReconsideringCybersecurity_Web.pdf

Lohrmann, D. (2018, September). *New national cyber strategy message: Deterrence through U.S. strength.* Government Technology. Retrieved from http://www.govtech.com/blogs/lohrmann-on-cybersecurity

Messdaghi, C., (2017, October). *Nonprofits cannot ignore cybersecurity.* [Web log comment]. Retrieved from https://blog.kennasecurity.com/2017/10/nonprofits-cannot-ignore-cybersecurity/

Middleton, B., Bloomrosen, M., Dente, M. A., Hashmat, B., Koppel, R., Overhage, J. M., . . . & American Medical Informatics Association. (2013). Enhancing patient safety and quality of care by improving the usability of electronic health record systems: Recommendations from AMIA. *Journal of the American Medical Informatics Association : JAMIA, 20*(e1), e2-e8. doi:10.1136/amiajnl-2012-001458

Mo, W., Zhu, S., Li, Y., & Kilper, D. (2017). *Dual-wavelength source based optical circuit switching and wavelength reconfiguration in multi-hop ROADM systems.* Retrieved from http://el2ne5ae7f.search.serialssolutions.com

Moultry, L. (2019). *10 Steps to working together in the workplace.* Small Business-Chron.com. Retrieved from http://smallbusiness.chron.com/10-steps-working-together-workplace-23055.html

Muck, S. (2012). Safeguarding PII on shared drives continues to be a challenge. *CHIPS Magazine, 30*(1), 13. Retrieved from https://www.hsdl.org/?view&did=11740

Nabi, A. (2017). *Comparative study on identity management methods using blockchain.* Retrieved from https://files.ifi.uzh.ch/CSG/staff/Rafati/ID%20Management%20using%20BC-Atif-VA.pdf

New York State Division of Criminal Justice Services. (2010, December 29). *Child sexual predators: The familiar stranger: DCJS releases video to help parents protect their children from sexual predators* [Video file]. Retrieved from http://criminaljustice.state.ny.us/pio/video/child-sexual-predators12-29-2010-hq.wmv

New York State Office of Information Technology Services. (2015-2016). *Protecting our children on the Internet.* Retrieved from https://www.its.ny.gov/keeping-kids-safe

Organization for Economic Co-operation and Development (OECD). (2001). *Science, technology, and industry scoreboard: Towards a knowledge based economy.* Paris, France: OECD.

Organization for Economic Co-operation and Development (OECD). (2011). *The protection of children online: Risks faced by children online and policies to protect them.* Retrieved from http://www.oecd.org/

officialdocuments/publicdisplaydocumentpdf/?cote=DSTI/ICCP/REG(2010)5/FINAL&docLanguage=En

Ostrowski, S. (2018, September). COMPTIA report examines the multi-generational workforce. CompTIA. Retrieved from https://www.comptia.org/about-us/newsroom/press-releases/2018/09/06/comptia-report-examines-the-multi-generational-workforce

Page, A., Hijazi, S., Askan, D., Kantarci, B., & Soyata, T. (2016). Research directions in cloud-based decision support systems for health monitoring using Internet-of-things driven data acquisition. *International Journal of Services Computing* (4), 18-34.

Peeking into the future by text mining: Zapaday, recorded future. (2011). Retrieved from http://datamining.typepad.com/data_mining/2011/09/peeking-into-the-future-by-text-mining-zapaday-recorded-future.html

Peltier, T. (2006). Social engineering: concepts and solutions. *Information Systems Security, 15*(5), 13. https://dx.doi.org/10.1201/1086.10658 98X/46353.15.4.20060901/95427.3

Ponemon Institute, LLC. (2017, May). *The impact of data breaches on reputation & share value :A study of marketers, IT practitioners, and consumers in the United Kingdom.* Centrify. Retrieved from https://www.centrify.com/media/4772757/ponemon_data_breach_impact_study_uk.pdf

Prayitno, A., Subanji, T., & Muksar, M. (2016, May-June). *Critical thinking decision refractive thinking with dual strategy in solving mathematics problem.* Department of Mathematics Education, Universitas Wisnuwardhana Malang, Indonesia Department of Mathematics, Universitas Negeri Malang, Indonesia. *IOSR Journal of Research & Method in Education (IOSR-JRME),* e-ISSN 232 –7388. Retrieved from https://www.academia.edu/29552493/Refractive_Thinking_with_Dual_Strategy_in_Solving_Mathematics_Problem

Reed, J. (2014, June 18). *How social media is changing language.* [Web log comment]. Retrieved from http://blog.oxforddictionaries.com/2014/06/social-media-changing-language/

Rosenbaum, M. H. (2015). *Identifying unethical personally identifiable information (PII) privacy violations committed by IS/IT practitioners: A comparison to computing moral exemplars.* Retrieved from ProQuest Dissertations & Theses Global. (UMI No. 1658171258)

Secureworks (2017, March 17). *Cybersecurity vs. network security vs. information security: Cybersecurity, network security and info security each serve a specific purpose in your security infrastructure.* Retrieved from https://www.secureworks.com/blog/cybersecurity-vs-network-security-vs-information-security

Shackelford, S. J., & Brady, A. E. (2018, January 12). *Is it time for a national cybersecurity safety board? Examining the policy implications and political pushback.* Albany Law Journal of Science and Technology, 2018. Kelley School of

Business Research Paper No. 18-34. Retrieved from https://papers.ssrn.com/sol3/papers.cfm?abstract_id=3100962

Sodiya, A. S., & Adegbuyi, B. (2016). A framework for protecting users' privacy in cloud. *International Journal of Information Security and Privacy (IJISP)*, 10(4), 33-43. doi:10.4018/IJISP.2016100102

Tabrizi, A. S. (2017). *Integrating cybersecurity education in K-6 curriculum: Schoolteachers, IT experts, and parents' perceptions* (Doctoral dissertation, University of Phoenix).

Tabrizi, A. S., & Lao, T. (2018). The refractive thinker®: Volume XV: Nonprofits: Strategies for effective management. In C. Lentz, (Ed.), *Managing nonprofit inevitable cyber-vulnerabilities* (pp. 69-80). Grayslake, IL: The Refractive Thinker® Press.

Tabrizi, A. S.., Sharifzadeh, M., Lao, T., & Paluch, E. (2018). The refractive thinker®: Volume XIV: Healthcare: The impact on leadership, business, and education. In C. Lentz (Ed.), *Health information technology: Critical-scrutiny of PII and PHI's Privacy - PII and PHI's privacy in a dynamic hyper-convergent world* (pp. 51-64). Grayslake, IL: The Refractive Thinker® Press.

Tapscott, D., & Tapscott, A. (2016). *Blockchain revolution*. Retrieved from http://blockchain-revolution.com

Tashakkori, A., & Teddlie, C. (1998). *Mixed methodology: Combining qualitative and quantitative approaches*. Thousand Oaks, CA: Sage.

Thakar, U., Varma, S., & Ramani, A. K. (2005). HoneyAnalyzer : Analysis and extraction of intrusion detection patterns & signatures using Honeypot. Retrieved from https://pdfs.semanticscholar.org/f4a4/6bc2447783164760f1318dd-ba7e82edd1989.pdf

The Levin Institute. (2014). *Information technology*. Retrieved from http://www.globalization101.org/information-technology

Tu, H. (2017, December). *From understanding telephone scams to implementing authenticated caller ID transmission*. Arizona State University. Retrieved from https://huahongtu.me/from-understanding-telephone-scams-to-implementing-authenticated-caller-id-transmission.pdf

Valdetero, J., & Zetoony, D. (2014). *Data security breaches: Incident preparedness and response*. Bryan Cave LLP. Washington Legal Foundation © 2014. Retrieved from https://www.bryancave.com/images/content/2/2/v2/2285/Data-BreachHandbookValdeteroandZetoony.pdf

Wawak, S. (2010). *The importance of information security management in crisis prevention in the company*. Cracow University of Economics. Retrieved from https://www.researchgate.net/publication/285158174

Wechsler, H. (2012). Biometric security and privacy using smart identity management and interoperability: Validation and vulnerabilities of various techniques: Biometric security and privacy using smart identity management and interoperability. *Global Issues in Context: The Review of Policy Research*, 29(1), 63-89. doi:10.1111/j.1541-1338.2011.00538.x

Wilkin, F. (2011, May 27). *Information weapons: Extreme news analytics from RecordedFuture*. Retrieved from http://www.programmableweb.com/news/ information-weapons-extreme-news-analytics-recordedfuture/2011/05/27

Zeadally, S., & Flowers, A. (2014, September 17). Cyberwar: The what, when, why, and how [Commentary]. doi:10.1109/MTS.2014.2345196. Retrieved from https://ieeexplore.ieee.org/abstract/document/6901336

Zopiatis, A., Krambia-Kapardis, M., & Varnavas, A. (2012). Y-ers, X-ers, and boomers: Investigating the multigenerational (mis)perceptions in the hospitality workplace. *Tourism and Hospitality Research*, 12(2), 101-121. http://dx.doi.org. contentproxy.phoenix.edu/10.1177/1467358412466668

About the Author . . .

Dr. Avideh Sadaghiani-Tabrizi is from the Capital Region in upstate New York and holds several accredited degrees: a Doctorate of Management (DM) in Organizational Leadership with Specialization in Information Systems Technology (DM / IST) and a Master of Science in Computer Information Systems (MS / CIS) from the School of Advanced Studies of the University of Phoenix. Dr. Avideh Tabrizi is an information technology security expert at the Office of Information Technology Services, Chief Technology Office – Enterprise Monitoring and Support Group, participating in monitoring, research, design, development, and maintenance of statewide network system with over 25 years of service at the New York State government. She enjoys travelling and likes to engage in various physical fitness activities when possible.

Dr. Avideh Tabrizi serves on North Colonie Central School District-Board of Education, participating in decision making, monitoring, and conducting reviews of the school district's curriculums, policies, and budget, in addition to serving as the president of high school's parents, teachers, and students' association. Her doctoral study entitled *Integrating Cybersecurity Education in K-6 Curriculum: Schoolteachers, IT Experts, and Parents' Perceptions,* provided her the opportunity to gain a deeper understanding about academic needs of children, to suggest and facilitate improvements in the school district.

To reach Dr. Avideh Tabrizi, please **e-mail:** avideh2012@yahoo.com

CHAPTER 5

Workplace Resilience Across the Ages

Dr. Rose Marie Whitcomb

Representation of diverse generations in the workplace demonstrates to employers that the best path to organizational success includes an inclusive workforce comprised of employees of a variety of ages and experiences. Workforce diversity includes a collection of individual attributes that together help to create a foundation allowing employers to pursue organizational objectives efficiently and effectively. Inclusion is achieved when employees feel valued for their unique qualities and abilities, and a sense of belonging develops (Hilman, 2014). Inclusive diversity exists when collaboration and unity evolves from a group of individuals successfully work together.

With five generations represented in today's workplace, the wealth of knowledge and experience at work is more expansive than in previous times. Yet developing a multigenerational and resilient workforce that remains engaged and motivated towards organizational goals, is a challenging task for employers. The successful management of generations blended into one workplace requires planning and skill to shape a workforce pulling together vs. apart. Organizations should direct the focus of employment practices towards inclusion as well as diversity (Hilman, 2014). Inclusion goes beyond the identification of differences–diversity. Refractive thinking in a workplace encourages employees to be expressive with their differences. An inclusive foundation at work provides individuals with the confidence necessary to express their differences in a safe and respected space. Successful organizations will plan for the inclusion of diverse groups within today's workplace, in addition to looking towards the growth of diversity opportunities in the future.

Generational bias involves prejudice either for or against individuals within an age cohort. Stereotyping creates limitations that prohibit a clear view of the multitude of ways individuals represent unique differences. Generational bias and stereotyping will stall progress and innovation while facilitating disengagement and distance between groups (Connell, Nankervis, & Burgess, 2015). Creating an inclusive environment for employees of all ages is an important step in maximizing the performance potential of all generations (Zemke, Raines, & Filipczak, 2000). Age is a number that does not necessarily accurately reflect a stereotypical label. Age is often a poor descriptor of a type of employee. Comments that may reflect age bias or stereotyping: *He's too young to step into that leadership position. At her age she may have difficulty keeping pace with the new technology. The seniors in our department may not be comfortable with our upcoming changes. He's too young to understand a work ethic.* Stereotypes linked to age carry the power to shape perceptions and build silos separating and stifling individuals and groups (Connell et al., 2015). When employers create an environment that values the skillset of a multigenerational workforce, skill, knowledge, and creativity spread throughout the workplace.

When employees experience inclusive acceptance of their unique contribution to the workplace, they are likely to value their work identity and respond to challenges in creative and innovative ways, which in turn provides for both organizational success and increased individual hardiness (Allred & Smith, 1989). A positive sense of work identity may contribute to the hardiness and resilience of the individual worker, as well as promoting the retention and tenure of the quality employee (Maddi & Khoshaba, 2005). A resilient work identity is likely to result when diverse age groups of employees reap benefit from opportunities available thru mentoring, skill enhancement, and exposure to generational difference.

Generations in the Workplace

For the majority of full time employees, time spent in the workplace surpasses time spent elsewhere. When surveying individuals in the United States with questions about their work and recreation activities, participants reported averaging 50 hours per week at work, two and one half times the amount of time spent on recreational activity (Reivich & Shatte, 2002). A similar polling in 1973 found the work to recreation ratio to be one and a half times (Reivich & Shatte, 2002). The overall number of hours that employees spend at work continues to increase, as does the number of years an individual remains in the workplace. Work is a predominant event filling an adult's time and this fact is not missed by employers. Identifying how best to make the experience of time at work rewarding for the individual employee, will in turn benefit the employing organization. Intergenerational conflict can negatively impact the employee population in a way that compromises the success of individuals and organizations (Zemke et al., 2000). Creating synergy within the multigenerational workplace will provide positive benefit to the individual employee's investment of time and is an important goal for organizational leadership.

Generations represented in the workplace may differ in their base of experience, including definition of work, interpersonal interactions, communication styles, and exposure to technology. Mentorship is one effective way to build and strengthen a multigenerational workforce while increasing a sense of value and appreciation for different perspectives (Anderson, 2019). Inclusive processes in the workplace will harvest the experience base of these different generations and provide learning opportunities to empower all employees to benefit from the richness derived from diversity. Individuals who participate in a mentorship experience may be more likely to appreciate what other generations bring to the workplace (Anderson, 2019). Exposure to generational differences may increase an understanding of unique attributes of individuals, which in turn can be critical in making diversity work for an organization and not against it (Zemke et al.,. 2000). In short, there is much to be learned from one another.

Millennials make up approximately 44% of the current workforce; in 2015, this age group surpassed the size of other generations represented in the workplace (Fry, 2015). Older workers may find benefit in reverse-mentoring as they seek opportunities to learn from the new and wider perspectives of their younger coworkers (Hilman, 2014). According to AARP's 2019 research, most employees report that they learn from their colleagues of different ages (Anderson, 2019). The workplace offers a rich environment for building a legacy of excellence for the younger majority, with an assumption that resilience through change is likely when individuals and systems find strength in learning from their differences.

Analysis of data from the Health and Retirement Study of 2005 indicated 80% of Baby Boomers anticipated working past the traditional retirement age of 65, at least part time (McNamara & Pitt-Catsouphes, 2013). This prediction certainly played out in reality more than 20 years later. Employees who find enjoyment in work, define their roles as being full of meaning and purpose and report an experience of engagement and satisfaction. These employees are likely to remain productive as they stay in the workplace longer (Cheung & Anise, 2012). Michelin Tire's company profile indicated 37% of the 22,000 employees and 80% of its senior management as being over the age of 50 (Grossman, 2013). The American Association of Retired Persons (AARP) (2013) reported that workers over the age of 50 have the highest retention rate of all age groups in the workplace and demonstrate the lowest absenteeism (Grossman, 2013).

Employers routinely devote time and resources in an effort to encourage and support diversity within their organization's workplace. Most frequently attention on diversity in the workplace is focused on ethnicity and gender. The most significant diversity challenge and opportunity in the workplace may be generational. Research on age diversity in the workplace demonstrated improved productivity and lowered turnover when a variety of age groups work together (Burch & Kelly, 2014).

As employing organizations adapt to the many generations of employees in the workforce, a variety of strengths and needs are identified. Assisting employees as they adjust to and accommodate the unique preferences and motivations of coworkers of other generations is an important task for organizational leadership. Poor management and under supporting generations of employees may result in reduced productivity in the workplace, disengaged employees and coworker teams, as well as increased conflict and decreased morale (Fry, 2015). Employers who demonstrate an investment in respect and appreciation for the unique value of each represented generation within the workplace are likely to reap the benefit of a more engaged and productive workplace.

The following are categories frequently used to describe generations in the U.S. workplace:

- Traditionalists (also known as Veterans and the Silent Generation)–born 1928 to 1945, approximate age 71-89, less than 2% of the current workforce.

- Baby Boomers–born 1946 to 1964, approximate age 53-70, 29% of the workforce.

- Generation X–born 1965 to 1980, approximate age 37-52, 34% of the workforce.

- Millennials–born 1981 to 1998, approximate age 20-36, 44% of the workforce.

- Generation Z–born 1999 to present, approximate age up to 18, less than 1% of the workforce. (Zemke et al., 2000)

Traditionalists within the United States stand out as the generation that views the workplace in terms of duty, honor and service. This generation's experience during the Great Depression and World War II demonstrated an appreciation for the opportunity to work, these employees entered the workforce during a time likely remembered for significant challenges.

Until 2015, Baby Boomers represented the largest generation in the workplace (Burch & Kelly, 2014). With a developmental span including the civil rights movement, a presidential assassination, the Vietnam War, and Woodstock; this generation benefits from questioning authority and speaking out to motivate change. Baby Boomers are a generation motivated by hard work with a willingness to invest the most time and energy in the workplace (American Management Association [AMA], 2007). Financial market upsets launching the recession of 2008 had a significant impact upon the retirement age of Baby Boomers and large number of these employees will work longer than what they had planned earlier in their career.

Generation X introduced the concept of work / life balance into the workplace. As the generation that matured during the era of technological advancement moving from landline to cell phone and from microfiche to Internet, dramatic change has shaped this age group. Often described as the most receptive to change, independent and internally driven, this generation seeks information with an expectation of near instant access. This generation also include the description as the *latchkey children* and the first group to experience a large number of households with two working parents. In addition to having experienced their years of development during a time of rapid change, this generation is likely to require the *why* behind instructions and to feel empowered to push through a rote response of *no* with a sense of confidence in questioning authority.

Millennials are known as the most highly educated, diverse and socially conscious generation in the workplace. This generation experienced memorable events perpetrated by both man and nature, including the Columbine shooting, 9/11, Hurricane Katrina, and the lengthy military engagements in Iraq and Afghanistan. Millennials experienced a lifetime that included Internet access and smart phone capability. Millennials are on track to soon comprise 46% of the U.S. workforce and 75% of the global workforce by 2025 (Burch & Kelly, 2014.) Millennial employees will continue to impact the workplace with their large numbers, as well as their motivation to facilitate change.

Generation Z enters the workforce as the future leaders who will be moving the workplace forward. As the youngest employees in the workplace, this generation is the least researched population to date (Stillman & Stillman, 2017). Employees in this generation may be the least tied to space and location as they have experienced a lifetime with wireless capability. As the horizon of employment progresses into an office-free era of remote work, unique challenges to work / life balance may begin. Being prepared to work wherever and whenever needed and also maintain a work / life balance may be a significant challenge for this generation to overcome.

A survey of literature specific to the tenured employee confirms the increasing age of the employee base in the United States. With the age of the average employee increasing, workers over the age of 50 represent one third of the U.S. workforce (Grossman, 2013). The maturation of employees in the workplace is significant in international studies as well (Gaillard & Desmette, 2010). Surveys of employers completed by the AARP (2013) indicated that workers over the age of 50 have the longest retention rate in the workplace, as well as the lowest level of absenteeism. The length of time in the workplace may provide an increased opportunity for developing and demonstrating resilience as an attribute of success (Ng, 2010). Moore (2012) provided evidence of how retaining resilient senior employees as role models and mentors for the next generation of workers offers a profitable return on investment (ROI) for the wise employer.

Ng (2010) completed a comprehensive literature review examining the role of age and attitude on work. The consistent finding of this research was evidence that older workers were most often found to display positive role modeling behaviors and were least likely to engage in counterproductive behaviors in the workplace (Ng, 2010). This review also found 60 studies reporting a positive correlation between age and job satisfaction (Ng, 2010). The use of role modeling and mentoring within the workplace are ways to successfully transfer vital information from generation-to-generation (Anderson, 2019). Employees who are less senior in age and time in the workplace may benefit from the tenure and experience shared by their more senior coworkers. This transfer of knowledge may be especially beneficial when optimism and resilience are demonstrated by the more senior employee in addition to sharing institutional and process information.

Stereotypes and Limitations

Generational bias may stall progress and innovation while facilitating disengagement and distance. Gaillard and Desmette (2010) provided extensive research on the existence of negative stereotypes of older workers. Employees over the age of 50 exposed to negative stereotypic information were more likely to retire early and were less likely to seek learning and development opportunities in the workplace (Gaillard & Desmette, 2010).

Achenbaum (2009) discussed the changes demonstrated in work ethic and life goals across generations. "The boomer's ultimate legacy will be to instill among citizens a sense of resilience and solidarity in the face of fragility and finitude" (Achenbaum, 2009, p. 96). When employers miss the opportunity of value and do not nurture their employees through the generations represented in the workplace, stereotypes and disengagement grow and this impacts performance and retention (Achenbaum, 2009).

In the United States, individuals spend much of their time as adults at work (Cheung & Anise, 2012). In addition to the increase in the amount of time per day, adults continue to work significantly longer in terms of total years invested at work. Retirement has evolved to a process that includes individuals continuing to remain in the workplace in some capacity in contrast to the past generations of completely leaving employment at a set age (Gaillard & Desmette, 2010). More time invested, more years accumulated, the workplace is all-encompassing in the life of employees. Maximizing the gifts of each generation represented at work will provide a wealth of opportunity to enhance the entire workforce. The first step in the direction of creating an inclusive incorporation of diversity of age in the workplace begins with an understanding of the experience of history of the generations represented in the workplace and how these experiences shape the culture of the multiple generations present.

Age of Resilience

A focused examination on workplace resilience specific to generation diversity begins with a concrete definition. "Fundamentally resilience is understood as a positive adaptation, or the ability to maintain or regain mental health, despite experiencing adversity" (Herrman et al., 2011, p. 258). If resilience develops as a result of facing and overcoming adversity with a positive outcome, then the employee group who demonstrates success within the workplace despite significant challenge, is worthy of study. As the workforce evolves to a multigenerational presence, much learning comes from employee groups of all ages.

In addition to the term *resilience*, research and writings focused on the workplace describe hardiness as an attribute of valuable employees (Maddi, 2005). Hardy individuals possess characteristics including (a) a sense of control over the future, (b) a sense of purpose, and (c) an attitude that identifies challenge as opportunity (Herrman et al., 2011). The workplace is an environment where a hardy employee has a sense of control and purpose, as well as a willingness to engage challenge with optimism. A resilient workforce, in turn, can create benefit to the bottom line: profit and success for the employer (Adams & Boehr, 1998). Because hardiness develops over time and with the experience with challenge, diversity of generations has much to offer the workplace.

In addition to the increasing amount of time invested in the workplace, challenge develops as a result of the level of stress present in the ever changing landscape of what is defined as *work*. Maintaining productivity and quality of work for the generations of employees in today's workplace requires an investment in the assessment, instruction, and enhancement of resilience in both the individual worker and the work group (Brooks & Goldstein, 2004).

Change is constant. The success of an employee and the employing organization requires strategy as well as a skill set that empowers individual and group resilience in the face of change. Employees and employers are expected to face unprecedented growth in technology and information in the future, while the level of competition in a global market will also increase. This trend will result in challenges for a diverse set of generations in the workplace, success moving forward will require a workplace with demonstrated hardiness and resilience (Maddi & Khoshaba, 2005). Resilience may be demonstrated differently across generations as the expression of recovery is likely a facet of the experience of the individual and the group.

With the inevitable forecast of change and challenge in the workplace, employers and employees of all generations will need to share a motivation to meet adverse circumstance with an optimism that sees the future as opportunity (Brooks & Goldstein, 2004). "Just staying above water does not insure that companies will thrive in rapidly changing, technologically innovative marketplaces. To thrive, companies and their employees must continually adapt and search for the potential opportunities within ongoing changes" (Maddi & Khoshaba, 2005, p. 179). Motivating work groups comprised of multigenerational diversity to embrace and accept change requires a skilled group of organizational leaders with sensitivity to the unique needs of the different generations represented in the workplace.

Change and challenge in the workplace have the potential to drain energy and momentum from both the individual employee and the employing organization (Ablett & Jones, 2007). One method for combating this drain is the infusion of resilient thought processes into organizational plans for change, as well as policies and procedures that manage the change from the perspective of optimistic opportunity (Maddi, 2005). When high levels of resilience and hardiness exist in an organization, employees will most likely endorse and comply with company change (Allred & Smith, 1989). When these constructs are low in the employee population, work includes a higher likelihood as simply a means to an end, or a necessary requirement to enable financial survival (Adams & Boehr, 1998). Creating a resilient and hardy workforce will in turn build a successful and enduring employing organization.

Literature suggested that both positive and negative results may be linked to age diversity in the workplace (Meulenaere & Boone, 2015). Positive results include the value added as knowledge and experience is enhanced by contributions from older employees. Negative results include the risk for conflict and challenge as cohesion is threatened by silos of individuals from diverse age groups (Meulenaere & Boone, 2015). Identifying and building resilience in the multigenerational workplace requires a change in focus for some organizations, especially those that have worked under a reactive and problem-resolution approach to personnel management. Inclusive change should include an examination of the rich resource a diverse workforce creates, acknowledgement of the successful coping skills of the tenured worker who has exemplified resilience and endurance in the face of workplace challenges, as well as appreciation for the innovative and creative and refractive thinking of the generations entering the workforce. In addition, employing organizations should build proactive programming to recruit, hire, support and retain individuals from a variety of generations with skills attributed to resilience.

Conclusion

The successful workplace includes acknowledgement and respect for difference. The refractive thinker will not be satisfied with silos of diversity but instead is driven to push for integration and inclusion as a variety of generations come together to thrive in today's workplace. The workplace is an environment with potential to enhance resilience of employees and reap the benefit from the opportunities that exist when individuals of a wide range of ages work together.

In summary, the steps for a successful multigenerational workplace should include: (a) facilitation of a culture that endorses diversity and inclusion, (b) an understanding that individuals differ and efforts to identify the strengths and preferences of each employee will result in a positive return on the investment of time and energy, (c) an ongoing assessment of bias and stereotypic reinforcement in the workplace, (d) frequent opportunities for education to identify the positive attributes and ideas of individuals and groups, (e) mentoring relationships across generations in the workforce, and (f) seeking feedback from employees to insure that diversity initiatives are adequate. Employing organizations benefit from the tenure of their workforce, and the wise employer invests in the facilitation of inclusion, coping skills and resilience in their employee base (Armstrong-Stassen & Ursel, 2009).

Life would be easier if resilience was acquired through osmosis, and not by surviving challenge and trial. But without the experience of hardship, success would not be as rewarding. Resilience is a byproduct of challenge and hardship that if not successfully resolved, has at least been faced and endured. When common traits in coping styles in the resilient employee are identified and quantified, an opportunity to create a more successful workplace develops. These attributes demonstrating resilience can be passed from one generation to the next building an enduring workforce with shared strength in overcoming challenge.

Research on the resilient workplace suggests that as individual employees progress through their career, they grow, change and become more competent with time and experience (Masten & Coatsworth, 1998). In addition, the presence of challenging experiences often results in the development of a more well-rounded and skilled employee, stronger following the experience of adversity, than they were prior to the event (Masten & Coatsworth, 1998). The employing organization that utilizes lessons learned from their tenured resilient workforce to enhance the hardiness of their other employee groups, will create an inclusive, well-rounded and successful workplace.

Enhancing resilience in the workplace, as well as creating inclusive processes focused on respecting diversity will require conscious decisions and dedication aimed at appreciating the unique skill set of individual employees. Generational diversity in the workplace is here to stay. The benefit of so many age groups working together at one time and in one space is an opportunity that should be embraced with optimism. Successfully managing and developing inclusive integration of diverse age groups within a workplace is the responsibility of both the employee and the employer. Tenured workers define the shape of an organization as they provide experience, guidance and demonstrated resilience to the workplace. New employees enter the workforce with enthusiasm and energy fueled by next generation ideas that will likely pave a path to an industry future that had only been visualized in the past. Seeing employees of all ages through the lens of their unique contribution will move the focus of the employer from one that sees a descriptive number, to an unprecedented level of clarity including a holistic view of a workforce honoring experience, ability, and resilience.

REFERENCES

Ablett, J. R., & Jones, R. S. (2007, December 14). Resilience and well-being in palliative care staff: A qualitative study of hospice nurses' experience of work. *Psycho-Oncology, 16,* 733-740. doi:10.1002/pon.1130

Achenbaum, W. A. (2009, Fall). A boomer at risk: A tale in personal, cohort, and historical perspective. *Journal of the American Society on Aging, 33*(3), 95-99. doi:10.1016/0531-5565(92)90054-4

Adams, G. A., & Boehr, T. A. (1998). Turnover and retirement: A comparison of their similarities and differences. *Personnel Psychology, 51,* 643-665. doi:10.1111/j.1744-6570.1998.tb00255.x

Allred, K. D., & Smith, T. W. (1989). The hardy personality: Cognitive and physiological responses to evaluative threat. *Journal of Personality and Social Psychology, 56,* 257-266. doi:10.1037/0022-3514.56.2.257

Anderson, O. G. (2019, January). Mentorship and the value of a multigenerational workforce. *Washington DC: AARP Research..* doi:10.26419/res.00270.001

Armstrong-Stassen, M., & Ursel, N. D. (2009). Perceived organizational support, career satisfaction, and the retention of older workers. *Journal of Occupational and Organizational Psychology, 82,* 201-220. doi:10.1348/096317908X288838

American Management Association (AMA). (2007). *Leading the four generations at work.* Retrieved from http://www.amanet.org/training/articles/ leading-the-four-generations-at-work.aspx

Bobek, B. (2002). Teacher resiliency: A key to career longevity. *The Clearing House, 75,* 202-206. doi:10.1080/00098650209604932

Boehm, S. A., Kunze, F., & Bruch, H. (2014). Spotlight on age-diversity climate: The impact of age-inclusive HR practices on firm-level outcomes. *Personnel Psychology, 67,* 667-704. doi:10.1111/peps.12047

Bursch, D., & Kelly, K. (2014). Managing the multigenerational workplace. *UNC Kenan-Flagler Business School, Executive Development, 2014.*

Brooks, R., & Goldstein, S. (2004). *The power of resilience.* New York, NY: McGraw Hill.

Cheung, F., & Anise, M. S. (2012, March). An investigation of predictors of successful aging in the workplace among Hong Kong Chinese older workers. *International Psychogeriatrics, 24,* 449-464. doi:10.1017/S104161021100192X

Connell, J., Nankervis, A., & Burgess, J. (2015). The challenges of an ageing workforce: An introduction to the workforce management issues. *Labour & Industry: A Journal of the Social and Economic Relations of Work, 25*(4), 257-264. doi:10:1080/10301763.2015.1083364

Fry, R. (2015). Millennials surpass Xers as the largest generation in U.S. labor force. *PEW Research Center*. Retrieved from http://www.pewresearch.org/fact-tank/2015/05/11/millennials-surpass-gen-xers-as-the-largest-generation-in-u-s-labor-force.

Gaillard, M., & Desmette, D. (2010). Invalidating stereotypes about older workers influences their intentions to retire early and to learn and develop. *Basic and Applied Social Psychology, 32*, 86-98. doi:10.1080/00098650432

Grossman, R. J. (2013, August). Invest in older workers. *Human Resource,* 20-25. doi:10.1037/0003-0453X.60

Herrman, H., Stewart, D. E., Diaz-Granados, N., Berger, E. L., Jackson, B., & Yuen, T. (2011). What is resilience? *La Revue Canadienne de Psychiatrie, 56*, 258-264. doi:10.1177/070674371105600504

Hilman, D. R. (2014). Understanding multigenerational work-value conflict resolution. *Journal of Workplace Behavioral Health, 29*(3), 240-257. doi:10:1080/15 555240.2014.933961

Maddi, S. R. (2005). On hardiness and other pathways to resilience. *American Psychologist, 60*, 261-262. doi:10.1037/0003-066X.60.3.261

Maddi, S. R., & Khoshaba, D. M. (2005). *Resilience at work*. New York, NY: MJF Books.

Masten, A. S. (2001). Ordinary magic: Resilience processes in development. *American Psychologist, 56*, 227-238. doi:10.1037/0003-066X.56.3.227

McNamara, T., & Pitt-Catsoupher, M. (2013). Employer policies for dependent care: The role of internal demographics. *Journal of Managerial Issues, 25*(2), 192-211. doi:10.14765/90432798543

Meulenaere, K. D., & Boone, C. (2015) Unraveling the impact of workforce age diversity on labor productivity: the moderating role of firm size and job security. *Journal of Organizational Behavior, 37*(2), 48-56. doi:10.1002/job2036

Moore, K. L. (2012, June). Building a robustness against ageism: The potential role of coaching and coaching psychology. *The Coaching Psychologist, 8*(1), 12-20. doi:10.1177/21582440124446

Ng, T. C. (2010). The relationships of age with job attitudes: A meta-analysis. *Personal Psychology, 63*, 677-718. doi:10.1111/j.1744-6570.2010.01184.x

Patrick, H. A. & Kumar, V. R. (2012, April-June). Managing workplace diversity: Issues and challenges. *SAGE Open*. doi:10.1177/2158244012444615

Reivich, K., & Shatte, A. (2002). *The resilience factor*. New York, NY: Three Rivers Press.

Stillman, D. & Stillman, J (2017). *Gen Z @ work*. New York, NY: Harper Collins Publishers.

Zemke, R., Raines, C., & Filipczak, B. (2000). *Generations at work*. New York, NY: AMA Publications.

THOUGHTS FROM THE ACADEMIC ENTREPRENEUR

The problem to be solved:

- How best to empower the refractive thinker® to create a resilient workplace that thrives with an inclusive mindset that authentically values the unique attributes of diverse generations of employees at work?

The goals:

- A focused examination of the value of diversity and inclusion of generations in the workplace demonstrating to employers that the best path to success includes a workforce comprised of employees representing a variety of ages.
- Examine the challenging task for the employers of today as they develop a multigenerational and resilient workforce that remains engaged and motivated towards organizational goals.

The questions to ask:

- What value does age diversity provide to the workplace?
- How will inclusion add depth and purpose to the experience of diversity in the workplace?
- What importance does resilience hold in the examination of generational differences in the workplace?
- What role will refractive thought contribute to the determination of success for 5 generations in the workplace?

Today's Business Application:

- A successful workplace includes acknowledgement and respect for difference. The refractive thinker will not be satisfied with silos of diversity but instead is driven to push for integration and inclusion as a variety of generations come together to thrive in today's workplace.
- Enhancing resilience in the workplace, as well as creating inclusive processes focused on respecting diversity will require conscious decisions and dedication aimed at appreciating the unique skill set of individual employees of all ages.

About the Author...

Dr. Rose holds a Doctorate in Psychology, is a Licensed Professional Counselor (LPC) in the state of Missouri and Kansas, is nationally recognized Certified Employee Assistance Professional (CEAP), Board Certified Counselor (NBCC) and Substance Abuse Professional (SAP), Dr. Rose maintains a goal of participating a lifetime of learning.

With several decades of work in the field of behavioral health, Dr. Rose developed programming for many organizations serving a variety of populations, including intensive in home family therapy with at risk youth, detention, and drug court services for juveniles, hospital based social services, and workplace employee assistance programs. Dr. Rose strives to remain current in research and program design as it pertains to the health, wellness, and productivity of the employee, family and the employer. Dr. Rose resides in Springfield Missouri with her husband of 36 years where she enjoys taking time to bask in the success of her adult children, as well as appreciating the new and ever increasing joy of her grandchildren.

To reach Dr. Rose Whitcomb, please **email:** rosewkids@aol.com

Strategies Used by Business Leaders to Reduce Employee Turnover in a Multigenerational Workforce

Dr. Borislav Perev, Dr. Alexandro Beato, & Dr. Denise J. La Salle

Reducing employee turnover is important to the survival of an organization. By studying current economic trends and increasing employee retentions, leaders can position their organizations to take advantages of forecasted economic growth in the geographical locations they serve. Business experts predict steady growth for the U.S. economy. To take advantage of the forecasted economic growth, leaders must be effective at managing a multigenerational workforce with a diverse level of professional experiences. A multigenerational workforce encompasses two or more generations. A generation is a distinct group sharing birth years, essential life experiences, and historical events (Lu & Gursoy, 2016). In the context of the place of work, these shared experiences effects employees' feelings toward authority and organizations' members (Lu & Gursoy, 2016). Therefore, generational differences are a force that can have a positive or negative impact on employee turnover. Understanding how to motivate a multigenerational workforce is essential to the success of an organization.

The unique characteristics from different generations may cause dissimilarities on how employees perceive and value their jobs; at the same time, these differences may affect other variables such as job satisfaction, work engagement, and turnover intention (Liat,

Mansori, Chuan, & Imrie, 2017). For instance, leaders of a service-oriented business must ensure employees behave courteously and exhibit proper behaviors. In addition, employees reported that working in a multigenerational workforce can be stressful because of the amount of time spent resolving issues and the intensity of those problems (Lu & Gursoy, 2016). Although managing employee turnover might be challenging leading a multigenerational workforce, when leaders create cohesive multigenerational teams, the benefits of such collaboration can lead to increased creativity and productivity.

Although a significant amount of research exists on employee turnover, most studies do not address the challenge of managing a multigenerational workforce. Currently, scholars and practitioners continue to hard to identify effective strategies to manage employee turnover in a multigenerational workforce. By exploring the literature, the goal is to provide recommendations on some effective strategies for managing a multigenerational workforce. By using a refractive thinking approach, leaders in a multigenerational workplace can gain new insights on effective employee retention strategies.

Background of Employee Turnover

Employee turnover is a problem that affects small and large businesses, which makes the situation subject for investigation (Al Mamun & Hasan, 2017). In addition, employee turnover creates challenges that influence the employee replacement process; at the same time, disrupts business operations (Al Mamun & Hasan, 2017). Wang et al. (2014) found that business leaders are facing challenges and losing money because of employee turnover as a result of leaders' inability to effectively manage a multigenerational workforce. According to Kim (2014), the costs of hiring new employees surpass the costs associated with an effective employee retention strategy. Therefore, senior leaders need to educate managers and supervisors on effective strategies to reduce employee turnover in a multigenerational workplace.

Business leader's need to identify an employee turnover strategy to promote not only the sustainability of the business, but also the retention of organizational knowledge (Alshanbri, Khalfan, & Maqsood, 2016; Rohde et al., 2015). Regardless of the field, leaders should try to identify signs of employee turnover intentions daily (Ferreira, Martinez, Lamelas, & Rodrigues, 2017). Employee turnover is a prevalent problem worldwide, and leaders need to work on findings solutions to any organizational challenge that might increase employee turnover intentions (Santhanam et al., 2015).

Managing employee turnover in a multigenerational workplace is vital to the overall success of the organization. Increased employee turnover has even a more significant effect on service-oriented businesses because of the relationships some customers built with some employees (Santhanam et al., 2015). The service industry is a customer service-oriented field and the success of an organization relies on the skills of employees to provide high-quality customer service. Consequently, the interaction between customers and employees affect the success of the business. Leaders looking for effective strategies to reduce employee turnover can benefit from adopting a refractive thinking approach.

Economic Impact of Employee Turnover

Business leaders must find ways to increase employee performance to achieve a competitive advantage; reducing employee turnover improves the overall performance of an organization (Wang, 2017). Service-oriented companies are the world's largest employers (Dipietro & Condly, 2007. Increased employee turnover has a significant impact on the success of service-oriented organizations;

failure to retain experienced employee can lead to organizational failure (Wang, 2017). The average employee turnover of service-oriented organizations is from 60% and 300% higher when compared to other business sectors (Dipietro & Condly, 2007).

Researchers failed to monitor and fully uncover the high costs of employee turnover (Guilding, Lamminmaki, & McManus, 2014). The costs of employee turnover vary; numerous variables affect such as the position and experience of the employee. For instance, a hotel with 30 front desk staff commanding a remuneration of $12 per hour, a 50% employee turnover level would generate $150,000 annual departmental costs (Hinkin & Tracey, 2008). An effective employee turnover strategy can lead to a reduction of organizational expenses as a result of lower employee hiring costs. Empirical evidence indicates that employee turnover is the primary cause of reduced productivity and profitability (Arbelo, Perez-Gomez, Gonzalez-Davila., & Rosa-Gonzalez, 2017). Scholars identified that increased employee turnover has a negative effect on job satisfaction, productivity, and hiring expenses (Arbelo et al., 2017; Jones, Hillier, & Comfort, 2016; La Salle & Beato, 2018). By improving a company's retention strategy, leaders can increase productivity and profitability in a multinational workplace.

In a competitive business world, employers need to take advantage of any opportunity to decrease costs (Aguenza & Som, 2018). Business leaders need to identify variables that affect employee turnover to increase the survivability of their organizations. Business leaders should implement practical business strategies and programs to reduce employee turnover and investigate the root cause of the problem. By implementing a viable employee turnover strategy, leaders can reduce employee turnover and gain a competitive advantage over competitors.

There is not a one-size-fits-all business strategy to reduce employee turnover. Instead, leaders need to understand the business sector they compete in and implement an employee retention strategy suited for their organization. Refractive thinking offers valuable strategies that can lead to a reduction of employee turnover in a multigenerational workforce. The best employee turnover reductions strategy considers the company's mission, vision, and employees' needs. Ultimately, an effective employee turnover reduction strategy should promote the retention of skilled and experienced workers who are vital to the success of the organization.

Current Status of Employee Turnover

A detailed look at the state of the economy is a reliable way to determine the status of employee turnover. Experts forecast steady growth for the U.S. economy during 2018 and beyond. Amadeo (2018), a senior-level corporate analysist and business strategist, forecasted the U.S. gross domestic product (GDP) would rise to 3.1% in 2018 and then to slow down to 2.0% by 2020. During the last quarter of 2018, the U.S. Bureau of Labor Statistics (BLS) reported an insignificant change in the number of job openings at 7.1 million and hiring employees reached up to 5.9 million, while the separations had an insignificant change to 5.6 million. The BLS indicated that within separations, the quits rate had also inconsequential change at 2.3%, where the layoffs and discharges rate remained static at 1.1%. The figures mentioned by the BLS and Amadeo indicate stabilizing economic landscape favorable for businesses' revival, which continues to create jobs and, keeping the employee turnover rates remain low.

Each generation has unique experiences that shape their professional behaviors and attitudes. Due to the last economic recession, employees for all generations with high or unique skills did not have the opportunity to work in their field of competence for quite some time. However, the U.S. GDP growth is favorable for the job market, which according to Amadeo (2018) contributed to the unemployment rate drop of 3.7% in 2018. The unemployment rate will remain flat at 3.5% in 2019 and 2020 (Amadeo, 2018). Besides, observation of data posted by the U.S. Bureau of Labor Statistics (BLS) (2018) indicated strong job growth in low-skills-low-pay sectors, such as retail and food service establishments. The recovery from the last economic resection took time, which led to an increase of structural unemployment, which Kahn (2015) depicted as the discrepancy between the available jobs and the skill levels of the unemployed. Respectively, although the BLS indicated relatively low employee turnover rates, as the economy continues to stabilize and businesses continue to hire, employees should consider looking outside their organizations for more favorable job offers, which in turn could additionally exacerbate the situation regarding employee turnover.

Effective Strategies to Reduce Employee Turnover

There is an ample amount of research on employee turnover is an effort by scholars and practitioners to find out more about the employee turnover phenomenon. However, based on their broader applicability and positive results, researchers emphasized some strategies more than other strategies. Employee job satisfaction and supportive leadership, and the interaction between both received an ample amount of attention.

Job satisfaction. When the employees feel satisfied with their job, the results are increased customer satisfaction, strong organizational performance, and improved employee retention (Nichols, Swanberg, & Bright, 2016). Organizational profitability might significantly improve with satisfied and productive employees (Amadeo, 2018). An increase in job satisfaction leads to employees experiencing a higher level of happiness at their jobs (Nichols et al., 2016). Happy employees also have a higher level of organizational commitment, which leads to low intentions for quitting the job.

Supportive leadership. Employees' positive perception of supportive leadership is a powerful factor used by employees to determine whether they stay on the job or leave an organization. Jehanzeb, Hamid, and Racheed (2015) found that when supervisory support drops even by a small index of 1.2%, the result could cause an escalation of employee voluntary turnover intentions by 37%. Effective management practices can induce employees to remain with companies because workers might perceive it as a supportive work environment and opportunities to grow and develop (Ma & Ghiselli, 2016). Shukla and Rai (2015) established that supportive leadership is a viable strategy to decrease employee turnover intentions.

Employee development. Savvy managers who recognize that supportive behavior helps uplift employees' motivation, improve job performance and reduce turnover investment, devote time and resources to employees' development (Karatepe & Vatankhah, 2014; Ma & Ghiselli, 2016). Effective processes for employees' realization of professional goals might be the reason an organization attracts and retains employees. Developments programs have a positive correlation with employees' job satisfaction and affect employees' turnover intentions negatively (Ma & Ghiselli, 2016). Organizations with effective employee development plans increase the retention of best performers because employees expect leaders' support with development and advancement opportunities (Karatepe & Vatankhah, 2014). An effective employee developmental strategy increases organizational commitment, promotes higher performance, and reduces turnover intentions.

Work engagement. Active promotion and enhancement of employees' work engagement are critical for the retention of valuable employees. Byrne, Peters, and Weston (2016) concluded that work engagement effect employee motivation because employees derive meaningfulness from work. Engaged employees exhibit affect, attention, and physical energy that triggers behavioral and attitudinal outcomes, such as increased job performance and organizational commitment. Employee engagement can generate a competitive advantage for the business, increase employees' productivity and business' profitability, and significantly influence employee turnover.

Fair treatment. When employees do not receive fair treatment, turnover is on the rise (Hwang, Lee, Park, Chang, & Kim, 2014), and management should explore different approaches to foster a climate of just throughout the organization (Moon, 2017). Unbiased treatment makes employees feel appreciated and valued, which intensify their sense of self-esteem and worth (Hwang et al., 2014). Fair employee treatment should go beyond the individual level, and organizational leaders must practice fair treatment on the corporate level that promotes an organizational justice climate.

Trust. Trust effects turnover because of mediating the relationship between leadership and employees' job satisfaction, organizational commitment, and psychological well-being (Ariyabuddhiphongs & Kahn, 2017). Trust between employees and managers make employees develop a higher propensity to take risks by introducing and implementing novel ideas. Managerial attributes, such as benevolence, ability, competence, and integrity, are indicative of the degree of trust employees could develop in their leaders (Nienaber, Romeike, Searle, & Schewe, 2015). Multi*generational leaders* must maintain trustworthy relationships with employees to sustain individual and organizational effectiveness because interpersonal trust is an essential antecedent of turnover.

Performance management coaching. The positive effect from coaching multiplies when managers devote their coaching efforts equally and continuously contribute to performance improvement of all employees, regardless tenure, experience, or career stage (Pousa, Mathieu, & Trépanier, 2017). Managing employees' performance should not be a boring paper-based task revisited every 12 months, but continuous coaching and feedback that motivates employees to deliver high performance throughout the year (Jones, 2016). When executed correctly, performance management coaching can significantly affect organizational performance by increasing employees' productivity, promoting professional development, and reducing turnover (Kalman, 2016).

Reward and recognition. Organizations with a variety of rewards and recognition programs are likely to sustain low organizational cost, increase organizational performance, and promote employees' job satisfaction. Equitable prioritization of rewards allocation that reflects the employee's output and contributions could be beneficial for businesses with high turnover and low organizational performance (Moon, 2015). Verbal compliments or small tangible rewards could build a feeling of organizational and collegial consideration, desirable to promote positive workplace behaviors (White, 2015). According to Moon (2015), satisfactory pay in the absence of recognition could be unsuccessful as a strategy to decrease voluntary turnover. Rewards and recognitions are a powerful and motivational strategy that organizational leaders should use to increase employees' engagement and reduce turnover.

Compensation. Employee compensation is an essential part of the organization's approach to rewarding employees. Competitive compensation is a strategic tool that employers can use to increase employee retention (Moon, 2015). Kwon (2014) concluded that a positive outcome from compensation packages that target an enhancement of employee output result in reduced voluntary employee turnover. Retention of workers for more extended periods will result in a skilled and committed workforce. Although compensation practices could be a complicated and frustrating part of the employee management system, a well-designed and implemented employee compensation is an effective way to reduce turnover and create a competitive advantage for the business (Pohler & Schmidt, 2016).

Leaders' Role in Creating a Culture that Promotes Employee Retention

The aggregation of multiple generations in the workforce creates a unique group of people that demands a strategic managerial approach to maintain low employee turnover. Leaders' role is of paramount importance for the effective handling of increased or continuous employee turnover. Scholars who studied leadership indicated that effective leaders might apply behavioral patterns associated with more than one leadership style (Dartey-Baah, 2015; Martin, 2017). Kang, Gatling, and Kim (2015) stated that employees often leave their job because they do not want to work for their current leaders. Managerial practices could affect the employee-employer psychological contract, affect employees' performance, and increase employee turnover intentions (Jung, Chan, & Hsieh, 2017; Wu & Chen, 2015). Effective leaders foster team cohesiveness and teamwork, which stimulates employees' job performance (Wang, Tsai, & Tsai, 2014), whereas ineffective management leads to increased employee turnover (Al Mamun & Hasan, 2017).

A dislike of leadership practices, such as workplace civility, could stimulate voluntary turnover. Rahim and Cosby (2016) determined that when workplace incivility is evident, employees are less productive and more likely to quit their jobs. Organizational leaders should elicit from employees' favorable behavioral responses that are beneficial for the organization's culture and business objectives jobs (Rahim & Cosby, 2016). Selecting applicants who are fit to work for the company is beneficial for the organization; even a small turnover difference lowers the organization's financial costs and increases its efficiency. Leaders are responsible for driving the success of their businesses, promoting employee engagement and commitment, and increasing employee retention and profitability. Using strategies found in this volume of *The Refractive Thinker*® can provide a strong foundation to build an organizational culture that promotes employee retention.

Consequences of Increased Employee Turnover

Employee turnover can have a devastating effect on the operation of a variety of business organizations, which made it a significant topic for exploration (Al Mamun & Hasan, 2017). Kaliannan and Adjovu (2015) shared that employee turnover cause more than a 32% profits reduction, and up to an 11% decline in earnings per share for some organizations. Selden and Sowa (2015) found that voluntary employee turnover along with other factors, such as tenure and expertise, the cost for replacing an employee may range from 50% to 200% of employee's salary. Research on employee turnover continued for several decades, which is an indication that this phenomenon remains a challenge for scholars and practitioners (Babalola, Stouten, & Euwema, 2016; Waldman, Carter, & Hom, 2015).

Increased employee turnover is a definite sign that organizations must improve retention policies; increased employee turnover leaders' ability to promote social change by costing organizations time, efforts, and resources. By reducing employee turnover, organizational leaders can sustain growth and profitability, improve the lives of employees and families, and better serve communities in which the companies operate. Tangible and intangible variables apply every time an employee leaves, and the turnover cost can be as high as the yearly employee wage (Inabinett & Ballaro, 2014).

High turnover rates can affect the bottom line for organizations because the cost of hiring new employees surpasses the cost of retaining current employees. Respectively, increased turnover has a negative effect on organizational profitability. Preventing employees from leaving must be a leaders' priority; retaining talent ensures sustainability, increases profitability, and enable leaders to meet stakeholders' expectations (Hausknecht & Holwerda, 2013; Martin, 2015). Organizational performance benefits from increased employee retention could elicit positive social change for the communities in which the organization operates.

Presentation of the Findings

After analyzing the findings of 50 recent publications on employee turnover, the agreement between researchers is that leaders of multigenerational workforces need to be adaptive. To effectively promote employee retention, multigenerational leaders need to use different leadership styles. Leaders must care about retaining employee because retaining experienced workers leads to increased productivity (Beato, 2017; Jehanzeb et al., 2015; La Salle, 2018). The review of the literature indicated three strategies that are effective when managing a multigenerational workforce: supportive leadership, reward and compensation, and effective communication. Below are the three recommended strategies for Refractive Thinker® readers wanting to reduce employee turnover at their workplace.

Theme 1: Supportive Leaders Reduce Employee Turnover

When leading a multigenerational workforce, another strategy that is effective is using a supportive leadership style. Supportive leaders do more than just telling employees what to do; supportive leaders check on their employees and make sure that workers have the resources and the skill to be successful. Supportive leaders enjoy delegating responsibilities to employees and use such opportunities to develop and mentor their followers. Supportive leaders know that they need to do more than tell their employees what to do. After assigning a task to employees, a supportive leader works with followers to assist them throughout the entire process. Researchers found that supportive leaders were effective at reducing employee turnover in a multigenerational workforce (Beato, 2017; Jehanzeb et al., 2015; Shukla & Rai, 2015). By using a supportive leadership style, leaders can reduce employee turnover intentions and lower the costs associated with hiring new employees.

The literature indicated that using a supportive leadership style reduces employee turnover because supportive leaders are more effective at gaining the trust of their employees (Ariyabuddhiphongs & Kahn, 2017; La Salle, 2018; Nienaber et al., 2015). Trusted leaders also improve job satisfaction, organizational commitment, and inspire employees to be willing to take evaluated risks (Ariyabuddhiphongs & Kahn, 2017). According to Ariyabuddhiphongs and Kahn, taking calculated risks can lead to increased productivity and improved profitability. Supportive leaders created an operating environment where employees are not afraid to make decisions (Nienaber et al., 2015). Supportive leaders build trustworthy relationships with employees and promote organizational effectiveness, as the result of an increase in employees' willingness to make decisions, growth in productivity, and a reduction of employee turnover intentions.

Theme 2: Adequate Compensation and Reward to Promote Retention

Offering competitive compensation is an important foundation when implementing an effective employee turnover reduction strategy in a multigenerational workplace. Another employee turnover reduction strategy that seems to work across all generations is offering adequate compensation to promote the retention of top performers. According to Moon (2017), leaders seeking for an effective strategy to reduce employee turnover should start with a review of employee compensations. Organizations that offer compensations equitable to the performance of its employees have lower turnover rates than organizations that do not offer competitive compensation (Beato, 2017; Moon, 2017). Although people in a generation share similar experiences that might affect how they perceive certain social issues; improving quality of life is one of the issues all generations are working toward (Pohler & Schmidt, 2016). Because people care about their quality of life, leaders need to ensure their organizations are compensating employees adequately.

Employees appreciate receiving acknowledgements from leaders for exceeding expectations. One effective strategy to show workers that the organization appreciates them for their hard work is offering rewards to recognize individuals who go above and beyond the call of duty (Moon, 2017). An effective reward program reduces employee turnover in a multigenerational workplace, improves organizational commitment, and increases job satisfaction. White (2015) found that organizations with reward programs were more effective at reducing employee turnover than organizations that failed to reward workers for their significant contributions. Another benefit associated with rewards is increased employee motivation (Moon, 2017). Organizations can set funds aside for leaders to use to reward top performers. When a leader notices someone doing an exemplary job, the leader can ask the reward program manager to buy a small gift. Rewards can be unique to each employee. For example, if a leader knows an employee likes coffee, the leader can request a $20 gift card to a coffee shop. By knowing the employee and making the reward personal, leaders have an even greater effect on employee turnover than buying just any gift. A reward program is an effective strategy to reduce employee turnover, and the benefits outweigh the costs.

Theme 3: Fair Treatment Decreases Employee Turnover

Fairness is an essential component of human resource management (HRM); however, fairness can mean different things to different people, which can lead to multiple interpretations. For example, some people might agree with the following statements while others might not: "Employees who have worked at a company for a long time deserve special treatment" or "Leaders should treat their employees based on their performance." Based on the previous statements, workers might understand fairness different based on their values, beliefs, and experiences. To effectively communicate with the employees where the organization stands on equal treatment, leaders need to provide guidance to employees in the form of policy letters and hold managers accountable in the implementation of those policies. When employees believe leaders are fair and unbiased, employees feel appreciated and valued, which in turn leads to increased self-esteem and worth and improved organizational commitment (Hwang et al., 2014; Moon, 2017).

When employees perceive leaders as fair, employees experience an increase in organizational commitment and productivity and a reduction of employee turnover intentions (Beato, 2017). By treating employees fair, leaders can have a positive effect on the performance of their organization, as the result of increased job satisfaction and trust. Treating employees fair is an effective strategy that works well in a multigenerational workplace because most people want their leaders to be fair-minded. The literature suggests that earning employees' trust is a significant mediator of employee turnover because people consider fair-minded leaders as trustworthy (Ariyabuddhiphongs & Kahn, 2017; Nienaber et al., 2015). In addition, when employees trust their leaders, employees are more willing to take an active role in the success of the organization. Reducing employee turnover should be a priority for all leaders. For an employee retention strategy to be effective, members of an organization need to perceive their leaders as trustworthy and fair.

Conclusion

Leaders need to find ways to retain top performers to gain a competitive advantage over competitors. Research indicated a link between employee turnover and supportive leadership, adequate compensation and rewards, and fair treatment (Hwang et al., 2014; Moon, 2017; Pohler & Schmidt, 2016; Shukla & Rai, 2015). Effectively reducing employee turnover in a multigenerational workplace is vital to the success of an organization. To increase the survival of their organizations in a competitive marketplace, leaders must take part in the implementations of effective employee turnover reduction strategies. As the literature indicated, leaders who support employees, use rewards to recognize superior performance, and treat their employees fairly have a positive effect on retention, organizational commitment, job satisfaction, organizational performance, and productivity. By implementing the strategies shared above and using a refractive thinking approach, leaders can effectively reduce employee turnover in a multigenerational workplace.

THOUGHTS FROM THE ACADEMIC ENTREPRENEUR

The problem to be solved:

* Reducing employee turnover in a multigenerational workplace
* Strategies for leaders to reduce employee turnover

The goals:

* Provide leaders with recommendations on effective strategies to reduce employee turnover in a multigenerational workplace
* Share insights on recommended strategies to reduce employee turnover

The questions to ask:

* Why should leaders care about implementing effective strategies to reduce employee turnover?
* What are some of the benefits of implanting an effective employee turnover reduction strategy?
* Is my organization retaining top performers effectively?
* What are the long-term effects of failing to reduce employee turnover?
* Do leaders in my organization know that generations are a unique group of people?

Today's Business Application:

* By implementing effective strategies to reduce employee turnover in a multigenerational workplace, the leader can increase job satisfaction, enhance productivity and profitability, and promote organizational growth.
* By dedicating organizational resources toward the retention of top performers, leaders are promoting a sustainable business practice.
* By reducing employee turnover, leaders have a positive effect on the survival of their organizations.

REFERENCES

Aguenza, B., & Som, A. (2018). Motivational factors of employee retention and engagement in organizations. *International Journal of Automotive and Mechanical Engineering (IJAME)*, *1*(6), 88-95. Retrieved from http://journal.ump.edu.my/ijame

Al Mamun, C. A., & Hasan, N. (2017). Factors affecting employee turnover and sound retention strategies in the business organization: A conceptual view. *Problems & Perspectives in Management*, *15*(1), 63-71. doi:10.21511/ppm.15 (1).2017.06

Alshanbri, N., Khalfan, M., & Maqsood, T. (2016). Retention of knowledge within the private sector organizations in the kingdom of Saudi Arabia. *Middle East Journal of Business*, *11*(3), 18-31. doi:10.5742/mejb.2016.92834

Amadeo, K. (2018). U.S. economic outlook for 2018 and beyond. Retrieved from https://www.thebalance.com/us-economic-outlook-3305669

Arbelo, A., Perez-Gomez, P., Gonzalez-Davila., E., & Rosa-Gonzalez, F. (2017). Cost and profit efficiencies in the Spanish hotel industry. *Journal of Hospitality & Tourism Research, 41*, 985-1006.

Ariyabuddhiphongs, V., & Kahn, S. I. (2017). Transformational leadership and turnover intention: The mediating effects of trust and job performance on café employees in Thailand. *Journal of Human Resources in Hospitality & Tourism, 16*, 215-233. doi:10.1080/15332845.2016.1202730

Babalola, M., Stouten, J., & Euwema, M. (2016). Frequent change and turnover intention: The moderating role of ethical leadership. *Journal of Business Ethics, 134*, 311-322. doi:10.1007/s10551-014-2433-z

Beato, A. (2017). *Effective strategies employed by retail store leaders to reduce employee turnover* (Doctoral dissertation). Available from ProQuest Dissertations & Theses Database. (UMI No. 10278363)

Boz, H., Yilmaz, O., Arslan, A., & Koc, E. (2016). A comparison of depression and turnover intentions of hotel employees in all-inclusive and non-all-inclusive hotels. *Global Issues and Trends in Tourism, 372-382.* Retrieved from https://www.researchgate.net/publication/311952159_Global_Issues_and_Trends_in_Tourism

Byrne, Z. S., Peters, J. M., & Weston, J. W. (2016). The struggle with employee engagement: Measures and construct clarification using five samples. *Journal of Applied Psychology, 101*, 1201-1227. doi:10.1037/apl0000124

Christ, K., & Burritt, R. (2017). Material flow cost accounting for food waste in the restaurant industry. *British Food Journal, 119*, 600-612. doi:

Dartey-Baah, K. (2015). Resilient leadership: A transformational-transactional leadership mix. *Journal of Global Responsibility, 6*(1), 99-112. doi:10.1108/jgr-07-2014-0026

Ferreira, A. I., Martinez, L. F., Lamelas, J. P., & Rodrigues, R. I. (2017). Mediation of job embeddedness and satisfaction in the relationship between task characteristics and turnover. *International Journal of Contemporary Hospitality Management, 29*, 248-267. doi:10.1108/IJCHM-03-2015-0126

Guilding, C., Lamminmaki, D., & McManus, L. (2014). Staff turnover costs: In search of accountability. *International Journal of Hospitality Management, 36*, 231-243.

Hausknecht, J. P., & Holwerda, J. A. (2013). When does employee turnover matter? Dynamic member configurations, productive capacity, and collective performance. *Organization Science, 24*, 210-225. doi:10.1287/orsc.1110.0720

Hinkin, T., & Tracey, J. (2008). Contextual factors and cost profiles associated with employee turnover. *Cornell Hotel and Restaurant Quarterly, 49*(1), 12-27.

Hwang, J., Lee, J. J., Park, S., Chang, H., & Kim, S. S. (2014). The impact of occupational stress on employee's turnover intention in the luxury hotel segment. *International Journal of Hospitality & Tourism Administration, 15*(1), 60-77. doi :10.1080/15256480.2014.872898

Jehanzeb, K., Hamid, A. B. A., & Rasheed, A. (2015). What is the role of training and job satisfaction on turnover intentions? *International Business Research, 8*, 208-220. doi:10.5539/ibr.v8n3p208

Inabinett, J. M., & Ballaro, J. M. (2014). Developing an organization by predicting employee retention by matching corporate culture with employee's values: A correlation study. *Organization Development Journal, 32*(1), 55-74. Retrieved from http://www.odinstitute.org

Jones, D. (2016). The future of performance management beyond appraisals. *Strategic HR Review, 15*(2), 100-102. doi:10.1108/SHR-02-2016-0008

Jones, P., Hillier, D., & Comfort, D. (2016). Sustainability in the hospitality industry: Some personal reflections on corporate challenges and research agendas. *International Journal of Contemporary Hospitality Management, 28*(1), 36-67.

Jung, C. S., Chan, H. S., & Hsieh, C. (2017). Public employees' psychological climates and turnover intention: Evidence from Korean central government agencies. *Public Management Review, 19*, 880-904. doi:10.1080/14719037.2016.1257060

Kahn, L. M. (2015). Skill shortages, mismatches, and structural unemployment: A symposium. *ILR Review, 68*, 247-250. https://dx.doi.org/10.1177/001979 3914564960

Kalman, L. (2016). Driving results through performance management. *Workforce Solutions Review, 7*(2), 22-26. Retrieved from http://www.ihrimpublications.com/ WSR_archives.php

Kaliannan, M., & Adjovu, S. N. (2015). Effective employee engagement and organizational success: A case study. *Procedia - Social and Behavioral Sciences, 172*, 161-168. doi:10.1016/j.sbspro.2015.01.350

Kang, H. J., Gatling, A., & Kim, J. (2015). The impact of supervisory support on organizational commitment, career satisfaction, and turnover intention for hospitality frontline employees. *Journal of Human Resources in Hospitality & Tourism, 14*(1), 68-89. doi:10.1080/15332845.2014.904176

Karatepe, O. M., & Vatankhah, S. (2014). The effects of high-performance work practices on perceived organizational support and turnover intentions: Evidence from the airline industry. *Journal of Human Resources in Hospitality and Tourism, 13*(2), 103-119. doi:10.1080/15332845.2014.847292

Kwon, H. S. (2014). Economic theories of low-wage work. *Journal of Human Behavior in the Social Environment, 24*(1), 61-70. doi:10.1080/10911359.2014.844615

La Salle, D. J. (2018). *Strategies for-profit educational leaders use to reduce employee turnover and maintain sustainability* (Doctoral dissertation). Available from ProQuest Dissertations & Theses Database. (UMI No. 10811668)

Liat, C., Mansori, S., Chuan, G., & Imrie, B. (2017). Hotel service recovery and service quality: Influences of corporate image and generational differences in the relationship between customer satisfaction and loyalty. *Journal of Global Marketing, 30*(1), 42-51.

Lu, A., & Gursoy, D. (2016). Impact of job burnout on satisfaction and turnover intention: Do generational differences matter? *Journal of Hospitality & Tourism Research, 40*(2), 210-235.

Ma, J., & Ghiselli, R. (2016). The minimum wage, a competitive wage, and the price of a burger: Can competitive wages be offered in limited-service restaurants? *Journal of Foodservice Business Research, 19*(2), 131-146. doi:10.1080/1537802 0.2016.1159889

Martin, J. (2017). Personal relationships and professional results: The positive impact of transformational leaders on academic librarians. *Journal of Academic Librarianship, 43*(2), 108-115. doi:10.1016/j.acalib.2017.01.012

Moon, K. (2017). Fairness at the organizational level: Examining the effect of organizational justice climate on collective turnover rates and organizational performance. *Public Personnel Management, 46*(2), 118-143. doi:10.1177/00910 26017702610

Nienaber, A. M., Romeike, P. D., Searle, R., & Schewe, G. (2015). A qualitative meta-analysis of trust in supervisor-subordinate relationships. *Journal of Managerial Psychology, 30*, 507-534. doi:10.1108/jmp-06-2013-0187

Nichols, H., Swanberg, J., & Bright, C. (2016). How does supervisor support influence turnover intent among frontline hospital workers?: The mediating role of affective commitment. *Health Care Manager, 35*, 266-279. doi:10.1097/ HCM.0000000000000119

Rahim, A., & Cosby, D. M. (2016). A model of workplace incivility, job burnout, turnover intentions, and job performance. *Journal of Management Development, 35*, 1255-1265. doi:10.1108/JMD-09-2015-0138

Pohler, D., & Schmidt, J. A. (2015). Does pay-for-performance strain the employment relationship?: The effect of manager bonus eligibility on nonmanagement employee turnover. *Personnel Psychology, 69*, 395-429. doi:10.1111/peps.12106

Pousa, C., Mathieu, A., & Trépanier, C. (2017). Managing frontline employee performance through coaching: Does selling experience matter? *International Journal of Bank Marketing, 35*, 220-240. doi:10.1108/IJBM-01-2016-0005

Rohde, P., Shaw, H., Butryn, M. L., & Stice, E. (2015). Assessing program sustainability in an eating disorder prevention effectiveness trial delivered by college clinicians. *Behaviour Research and Therapy, 72*, 1-8. doi:10.1016/j.brat.2015.06.009

Santhanam, N., Kamalanabhan, T., Dyaram, L., & Ziegler, H. (2015). Examining the moderating effects of organizational identification between human resource practices and employee turnover intentions in India hospitality industry. *GSTF Journal on Business Review (GBR), 4*(1), 11-19.

Selden, S. C., & Sowa, J. E. (2015). Voluntary turnover in nonprofit human service organizations: The impact of high performance work practices. *Human Service Organizations: Management, Leadership & Governance, 39*, 182-207. doi:1 0.1080/23303131.2015.1031416

Shukla, A., & Rai, H. (2015). Linking perceived organizational support to organizational trust and commitment: Moderating role of psychological capital. *Global Business Review, 16*, 981-996. doi:10.1177/0972150915597599

Solnet, D., & Kralj, A. (2011). Generational differences in work attitudes: Evidence from the hospitality industry. *Hospitality Review, 29*(2), 37-54. Retrieved from https://digitalcommons.fiu.edu/hospitalityreview/vol29/iss2/3

U.S. Bureau of Labor Statistics (BLS). (2015). *Job openings and labor turnover survey news release.* Retrieved from http://www.bls.gov/news.release/jolts.htm

U.S. Bureau of Labor Statistics(BLS). (2018). *Job openings and labor turnover-October 2018.* Retrieved from http://www.bls.gov

Waldman, D. A., Carter, M. Z., & Hom, P. W. (2012). A multilevel investigation of leadership and turnover behavior. *Journal of Management, 41*, 1724-1744. doi:10.1177/0149206312460679

Wang, C. J., Tsai, H. T., & Tsai, M. T. (2014). Linking transformational leadership and employee creativity in the hospitality industry: The influences of creative role identity, creative self-efficacy, and job complexity. *Tourism Management, 40*, 79-89. doi:10.1016/j.tourman.2013.05.008

White, P. (2015). Appreciating your staff makes sound business sense. *Human Resource Management International Digest, 23*(2), 31-33. doi:10.1108/ hrmid-01-2015-0014

Wu, C. M., & Chen, T. J. (2015). Psychological contract fulfillment in the hotel workplace: Empowering leadership, knowledge exchange, and service performance. *International Journal of Hospitality Management, 48*(1), 27-38. doi:10.1016/j.ijhm.2015.04.008

About the Authors...

Dr. Borislav Perev resides in Kissimmee, Florida and currently works for The Walt Disney Company. Additionally, Dr. Borislav is an adjunct faculty member at Bellevue University. He and his family moved to the United States back in 2005 and in 2013 became naturalized U.S. citizens. Dr. Borislav received a Doctor of Business Administration (DBA) in Leadership from Walden University in 2018 and in 2011, a Master of Business Administration (MBA) with majors in Management, and Hospitality and Tourism Management from Strayer University. In 2012, he also completed an executive certificate in Business Administration with an emphasis on Human Resources Management (HRM) from Strayer University. In his time off, he explores new business trends and looks for opportunities to exchange ideas and expertise with friends and peers. He is passionate about researching organizational psychology, corporate performance, leadership approaches, employee turnover and retention strategies, and organizational success factors.

Dr. Borislav is also an active member of Alpha Chi National College Honor Society, Golden Key International Honor Society, and Sigma Alpha Pi National Society of Leadership and Success.

His doctoral dissertation, *Strategies Hospitality Leaders Use to Reduce Employee Turnover,* was published in the digital ProQuest Dissertation & Thesis Global™ Database.

To reach Dr. Borislav Perev, please contact him by **email** at dr.bperev@gmail.com

Dr. Alexandro Beato resides in El Paso, Texas with his wife and three children. Dr. Alexandro is currently an adjunct professor at Park University and Webster University. He retired from the U.S. Army in 2015. Dr. Alexandro received a Doctor of Business Administration (DBA) in healthcare management from Walden University in 2017 and a Master of Business Administration (MBA) in marketing from Columbia Southern University in 2011. He also completed a master certificate in Lean Six Sigma from Villanova University in 2018. Dr. Alexandro also serves as a senior dissertation editor for Editors Dissertations and Thesis. In his time off, he enjoys mentoring and coaching students with their dissertations and helping them achieve their educational goals. He is passionate about researching organizational leadership, employee turnover, corporate performance, and employee retention.

Dr. Beato is also an active member of The Delta Mu Delta Honor Society, The Golden Key International Honor Society, and The National Society of Leadership and Success.

Dr. Alex is a best-selling author. He previously collaborated in two chapter to help increase understanding on employee turnover in the healthcare industry. In *The Refractive Thinker: Vol XIV: Healthcare: The Impact on Leadership, Business, and Education* and *Vol XV: Nonprofits: Strategies for Effective Management*. He has published two journal publications: *Implementing Effective Strategies to Reduce Employee Turnover: Retail Managers Share Experiences* and *Successful Strategies Leaders Use to Reduce Employee Turnover and Maintain Sustainability in For-Profit Colleges*. Additional work includes his dissertation: *Effective Strategies Employed by Retail Store Leaders to Reduce Employee Turnover*, which is available from the ProQuest Dissertation & Thesis Database.

To reach Dr. Alexandro Beato for information on refractive thinking, professional editing, or guest speaking, please contact him by **email** at alexbeato1@ yahoo.com

Dr. Denise J. La Salle resides in Orlando, Florida with her husband. She has three boys and two grandchildren. Dr. Denise is an adjunct professor at a local college. Currently, she owns and manages a used tires retail shop. Also, she opened three non-profits: The La Salle Educational Foundation, International Books of Hope, and Adopt a Teacher Foundation. Her vision is to open bilingual schools in foreign countries for less privileged people. Dr. Denise is in the process to open the first school and library in Bolivia. Her philosophy is *"I cannot change the world, but I can change the world of someone through education."*

Dr. Denise received a Doctor of Business Administration (DBA) in International Business from Walden University in 2018, a Master in Educational Leadership from Ana G. Mendez University in 2010, and a Bachelors in Elementary Education from Interamerican University of Puerto Rico. Recognized as a STAR teacher for excellence in teaching, she was also recognized as in the top 25% teachers in Orange County, Florida. She received a recognition letter from the President of the United States in 2007 for her commitment to education. In 2019, Dr. Denise was interviewed in a live radio show named *Silver Lining in the Cloud* on Business RadioX in Atlanta Georgia to promote her nonprofits. In her time off, she enjoys spending time with her grandchildren and traveling with her husband.

She has published two journal publications and one chapter book.

La Salle, D. (2018). Strategies for profit educational leaders use to reduce employee turnover and maintain sustainability (Doctoral dissertation). Available from ProQuest Dissertation & Thesis Database.

La Salle, D., Beato, A., & Velkova, G. (2018). Successful strategies used by leaders to reduce employee turnover and maintain sustainability in for-profit colleges. The International Journal of Business & Management. Retrieved from http://www.theijbm.com

La Salle, D., & Beato, A. (2018). Strategies to reduce employee turnover in nonprofit higher education. In the Refractive Thinker®: Vol XV: Nonprofits: Strategy for effective management (pp. 105-130). Las Vegas, NV: The Refractive Thinker® Press.

To reach Dr. Denise J. La Salle, please contact her by **email** at laedfo@ yahoo.com

Towards a New Paradigm of Management with Algorithms, Automation, and Artificial Intelligence

Dr. Nsikak Akpakpan

Since 1900, the practice of management has stood the test of time, responsible for the success of the business enterprise in creating wealth for its owners, employment for people, value for the customers, and prosperity for Nations–the hallmark of political stability and engagement (Estes, 2019). The endeavor of management started as an innocent attempt at the design of work to minimize the labor cost (Ng, 2011; Ribeiro & Gomes, 2016). Management blossomed into the philosophy of societal prosperity through commerce, from the ruthless pursuit of labor efficiency in the pre-Taylorism era to the use of cognitive computing to elevate human activity to democratize business efficiency for sustainable production and consumption. The evolution of management thinking followed Kuhn's 1962 paradigm shifts, starting with the labor-management paradigm, through scientific management, information systems management, data analytics management to so-called cognitive management paradigm (as cited in Khorasani & Almasifard, 2017; Mortenson, Doherty, & Robinson, 2015). The management paradigm shifts paralleled changes in the theories of organization, decision making, and information (Burke, 2017; Tsoukas, 2017).

The paradigm shifts also correlated with advances in technology which made the Internet, communication protocols, distributed applications, cloud databases, online global communities, multinational commerce, and online marketplaces, to name a few, plausible digital business models (Leonardi, Levina, Truelove, & Vaast, 2018; Wang, Chaudhry, & Da Xu, 2016). The management thinking needed to guide these new digital business models should be different from those that have so far been effective. Given this complexity of business processes and models, unaided human deconstruction of the business activities into the underlying causal relationships for dependable decision-making is no longer feasible, even for highly experienced and older managers and executives (Piaskowska, Nadolska, & Barkema, 2017; Williams, 2016). The Silent and Baby Boomer generations, who hold a disproportionate number of executive and top-management positions in companies in mature industries have the most challenging time with the cognitive management paradigm. The middle-aged and younger generations (Gen X, Y, and Z) welcome and leverage the cognitive management transition as the ladder to the executive suite (Ansoff, Kipley, Lewis, Helm-Stevens, & Ansoff, 2019; Mol & Birkinshaw, 2009). Generational diversity in the executive suite is an essential driver for the new business wave and transformations to automation, algorithms, and artificial intelligence augmentation of human capabilities for sustainable efficiency in managing businesses (Beneventi, 2018; Urick, 2019).

This chapter is a refractive thinking examination of the cognitive paradigm of management to highlight challenges and the opportunities regarding information representation and the strategies for the multigenerational workforce. The next section covers the historical journey of the practice of management and the rationale for a new paradigm of management supported by algorithms, automation, and artificial intelligence. The goal is to discuss the information capabilities needed to take advantage of the evolution in the management of transactions of organizations, and the solutions to minimize failures. The questions to ask are how organizations can improve the results of investments to achieve the promise of intelligent business entities. The last section of this chapter covers the evaluation of the cognitive paradigm of management in the context of a multigenerational workforce with disparities in managerial roles and digital skills, considering the shift in the decision-making locus away from the older, more experienced, less technologically savvy executives to the younger, less experienced, more technologically savvy managers and workers.

The Evolution of Management Thinking

A historical journey of management practices is necessary to under-stand how the cognitive paradigm of management came about, based on a template from Mortenson, Doherty, and Robinson (2015). Management started as an attempt to design work to min-imize labor cost (Ng, 2011; Ribeiro & Gomes, 2016). The designs of the work created roles and responsibilities and the workflow mechanized to substitute labor (Daft, 2015; Ingvaldsen, 2015). However, for this to be profitable, there needed to be significant increase in the production capacity; management thinking evolved into specialization of tasks, division of labor, assembly lines, and mass production that made up the labor-management paradigm of the industrial era (Kochan, Riordan, Kowalski, Khan, & Yang, 2019). Manufacturing plants required significant investments to build, processes to ensure the availability of raw materials needed for production and the distribution for the products. Organiza-tional theories such as transaction cost theory drove the design of work and organizations, and Adam Smith's (1776) thinking pro-vided the blueprint for the practice of management (as cited in Smith & Wilson, 2019). New technologies begot new products, services, and industries. These new technologies impacted physical labor and methods of production, but with a singular focus on capacity and not much on quality. Management thinking remained in this paradigm until early 1900 (Mortenson et al., 2015).

The scientific management paradigm started about 1910 with the publication of *The Principles of Scientific Management* by Frederick Winslow Taylor. World War II added urgency to the evolution of management to address the unique demands, which led to the discovery of the first programmable digital computer by Alan Turing and development of novel quantitative methods of operational research to support the British war effort (Ceruzzi, 2003; Mortenson et al., 2015). After the war, significant advances occurred in commercial computing, including the von Neumann architecture which divided processing from memory storage, programming languages like FORTRAN, COBOL, and the UNIVAC computer, which successfully predicted the 1952 presidential election (Ceruzzi, 2003; Donaldson, 2016).

The technological advancements led managers to focus on the use of scientific methods like the design of experiments, hypothesis generation, and hypothesis testing to drive the understanding of cause and effect relationships within the business environment (Andraszewicz et al., 2015; Mortenson et al., 2015). The absence of significant amounts of data meant the solution of management problems had to involve mathematical methods like linear programming, integer programming, and other early discoveries in operations research (Hazen, Skipper, Boone, & Hill, 2018; Mortenson et al., 2015). Statistical methods helped managers to get insights with limited data, and to be able to extrapolate the interpretation of results gathered on a small number of subjects to a larger population (George, Osinga, Lavie, & Scott, 2016; Mortenson et al., 2015). The scientific management practices remained popular until the mid-1960s when computers became more accessible to businesses, which heralded the Information Systems paradigm of management (Eroshkin, Koryagin, Kovkov, Panov, & Sukhorukov, 2017; Mortenson et al., 2015).

The information systems paradigm of management saw the transformation of computers into information systems through advances in hardware and software (Legner et al., 2017; Schwab, 2017). Information systems replaced the filing cabinet, and advances deepened integration into business processes, which allowed more data capture about the activities of the business. Specialized computers, such as RASCEL, solved stochastic methods which were time and resource intensive for businesses. Further development of specific systems to support management, so-called, management information systems followed (Mortenson et al., 2015). However, the new management information systems were only capable of presenting very static information, often in printed form, and the gap in the potential of the systems and the value proposition for analysts and managers widened (Shiau, Chen, & Tsai, 2015). The attempt to close this gap led to the development of better systems to help management as expert systems and decision support systems (Ansoff, Kipley, Lewis, Helm-Stevens, & Ansoff, 2019; Ross, 1976).

Expert systems provided suggestions based on the specific circumstances of the decision using the rules defined in them while decision support systems were much more general and used relevant data from model results (Ansoff et al., 2019; Tekez, 2018). This period saw the convergence of developments in technology, quantitative methods, and decision-making into a new discipline of Decision Science (Kleindorfer, Kunreuther, Kunreuther, & Schoemaker, 1993; Sengupta, Gupta, & Dutta, 2016). Decision methodologies, such as Multicriteria Decision Analysis (MCDA), Analytical Hierarchical Process (AHP), and other emerged as the basis for combining subjective and objective criteria into the solution of decision problems (Ariño, de Santiago, & Seager, 2017; Branke, 2016). The classical decision problem is a 4-tuple, made up of actions, alternatives, consequences, and preferences, solvable by enumerating and quantifying each of the tuples (Ma, Jiang, Liu, Luo, & McGreevy, 2018).

In the absence of data, these methods had to settle for weights and rates that are qualitative, hence, the standard reference to them as soft methodologies (Martinez, Rodriguez, & Herrera, 2015). Two key advances in this period were (a) information theory by Claude Shannon with the publication of *Mathematical Theory of Communication* and (b) database theory by Edgar F. Codd with the publication of *A Relational Model of Data for Large Shared Data Banks* (Mortenson et al., 2015). The advances along with the tools and technology like Structured Query Language (SQL), Relational Databases, Relational Data Models, to name a few, heralded the data analytics paradigm of management (Chen & Bai, 2017; Sułkowski & Kaczorowska-Spychalska, 2018). Organizations invested in many information systems at the end of this period causing the issue of data silos and information integration.

The need to advance management analytics demanded solution to data silos and led to the new data technological discoveries including Extract, Transform, and Load (ETL) tools, Multidimensional data modeling, the Online Analytic Processing (OLAP) tool, and new architecture for so-called data warehouses - collections of data from organization's information systems to centralize integration, standardization, and rationalization (Boutkhoum & Hanine, 2017; Kimball et al., 2008). With this foundation, the concept of business intelligence systems arose as the application interfaces into data warehouses, which led to new management concepts, such as key performance indicators, metrics dashboards, and balanced scorecards, that convey the state of business performance (Harvey & Sotardi, 2018; Irene, Marika, Giovanni, & Mario, 2016).

Business intelligence systems established the architectures needed to democratize analytic processes and deliver insights to support decision making (Chandra & Gupta, 2018). Unfortunately, advancement of the Internet with drastically new business models and capability to capture massive amounts of data meant rethinking of the business intelligence systems approach to management support (Hazen, Skipper, Boone, & Hill, 2018).

Accumulation of data led to the broadening of business analytics from the mid-2000s to support the realization of value from the massive amount of data, so-called big data (Schildt, 2017; William, 2016). The nature and complexity of the data forced the introduction of new technologies including Hadoop, MapReduce, NoSQL, NewSQL, Platforms with API data streams, such as Facebook, Twitter, and others (Mohanty, Jagadeesh, & Srivatsa, 2013, William, 2016). Also, big data and digital business ecosystems, such as Amazon, Facebook, Google, and others, formed (Hewage, Halgamuge, Syed, & Ekici, 2018). Simple predictive analytics of the typical business analytics system could no longer support decisions in this environment. The need for more sophistication heralded the next paradigm discussed in the next section.

Cognitive Paradigm of Management

The previous section provided the historical basis for the evolution of the practice of management to the current state, the cognitive paradigm of management. Today, data inundates most businesses, and investing strategically to extract value from data for internal business process improvement and new streams of revenue is popular (Grover, Chiang, Liang, & Zhang, 2018; Thomas 2016). The drive is to manage the discovery, validation, and operationalization of insights embedded in the available data (Haupt, 2018). The cognitive management approach gained attention in 2011 after IBM Watson won jeopardy (Gupta, Kar, Baabdullah, & Al-Khowaiter, 2018). A review of the literature indicates the three periods in the development of this paradigm followed one another in very rapid succession, the first being the rise of analytic algorithms: data mining, machine learning, and deep learning which led to the formalization of the discipline of Data Science (Frank, Roehrig, & Pring, 2017). The second was the rekindling of process automation initially focused on robotic processes but evolved quickly to cognitive processes (Lacity, & Willcocks, 2018: Mendling, Decker, Richard, Hajo, & Ingo, 2018). The most recent is the rise of self-organizing groups and distributed autonomous organization (Richard, Hajo, & Ingo, 2018; Swan, 2015, 2018).

Data mining, machine learning, and deep learning compose of families of analytic algorithms that facilitate the discovery, extraction, and application of patterns from big-data in decision making. Analytic algorithms came with the concept of model, which is a set of logic that produces one or more output values given a set of inputs, transforming data analysis into the process of building the models that represent associations within the input data (Witten, Frank, Hall, & Pal, 2016). For example, genetic algorithms and neural networks models high dimensional and dynamically discontinuous processes, while memory-based rea- soning models reasoning based on the information carried in sam- ple cases (Witten et al., 2016). With the analytic algorithms, the opportunity is in managing the models of associations embedded in the data and making the results available for decision making (Kumar, McCann, Naughton, & Patel, 2016). The nature of avail- able data demanded significant manual effort in preparing the data for the analytic algorithm which highlighted the need for process automation capabilities (Kanter & Veeramachaneni, 2015; Rah- man & Rutz, 2019).

Process automation which started with the focus on manual or robotic processes soon expanded to include other strategies of automation from simple data integration processes to complex reasoning and inference problems requiring artificial intelligence capabilities. The combination of automation and analytics is responsible for the creation of autonomous objects, the most nota- ble being self-driving cars, and self-flying drones (Ayoub & Payne, 2016; Russell, Hauert, Altman, & Veloso, 2015). With process automation, many tedious management tasks can be automated and tracked (Ayoub & Payne, 2016). The role of the manager changes to ensuring the appropriate enhancements are made to the automated process to maximize accuracy, and present alternative scenarios that cannot be digitally derived based on the data available (Geyer-Klingeberg, Nakladal, Baldauf, & Veit, 2018; Veit, Geyer-Klingeberg, Madrzak, Haug, & Thomson, 2017). Advances in the use of algorithms and automation to drive management actions has got to a point in which the overhead of management and organization has started to drive a change that may finally end business enterprises and the practice of management as we have come to know them (Mendling et al., 2018; Swan, 2018).

As of 2019, management practice revolves around the nurturing the digital workforce to deliver the cognitive capabilities for the global marketplace (George, Osinga, Lavie, & Scott, 2016; Peng, 2017; Sherman, 2019; Swan, 2018). Consider the most recent advancement in transaction management, blockchain protocol, which promises companies without managers, countries without politicians, and markets without any intermediaries (Sherman, 2019; Swan, 2018). The first implementation of the blockchain protocol was Bitcoin, a global currency without a Central Bank manager, and all transactions go through governance and verification by consensus with secure computer programs, so-called, smart contracts (Sherman, 2019). The developers of the smart contracts earn from work done to verify and govern transactions on the Bitcoin network, so-called Bitcoin mining (Christidis & Devetsikiotis, 2016; Yermack, 2017). Bitcoin miners are completely decentralized, but the consensus protocol ensures consensus before addition of a transaction to the chain. The Bitcoin network is the distributed autonomous organization (DAO) for the management of transactions with bitcoin, utterly devoid of intermediaries, for now (Swan, 2018; Tapscott & Tapscott, 2016). Other DAOs are forming on many industries to disrupt the powerful intermediary organizations like Google, Amazon, Uber, and others (Sherman, 2019; Swan, 2018). DAOs form just-in-time to execute a transaction between two or more parties, as opposed to modern organizations that aggregate transactions to minimize the overhead cost per transaction (Christidis & Devetsikiotis, 2016; Yermack, 2017) The foregoing underscores the importance of a robust solution architecture that combines the business, application, data, and infrastructure models of the organization is paramount to advance cognitive capabilities. The next section discusses such solution architecture formulations to support the cognitive management paradigm.

Cognitive Management Paradigm Solution Architecture

This section covers the solution architecture for the cognitive management paradigm. This solution architecture is based on observation and reporting that investments in data analytics projects which is intended to facilitate cognitive enablement typically failed to deliver acceptable and actionable results to business end users, with a cost of as much as $2.7 trillion in 2016 for companies in the United States (Gartner Inc, 2016). An examination of the data model of a typical such project, as well as the project management approach, identified some of the reasons why these projects failed (Akpakpan, 2018).

The critical reason for the failures was that fundamental changes in requirements demanded drastically new approaches (Akpakpan, 2018; Kassarnig & Wotawa, 2018a, 2018b). Analytic data modeling for most failed data analytics projects followed the classical multidimensional modeling. The multidimensional data models have facts and dimension entity relations, but research indicated issues with the approach particularly with big data, such as heterogeneous and irregular dimensions, handling of different types of aggregation operations, handling time and uncertainty, symmetrical treatment for dimension and fact elements, and support for different levels of granularity in the facts and dimensions, among others (Bertossi & Milani, 2018; Moukhi, Azami, & Mouloudi, 2018).

The functional form expression of subject underlying the data was required to formalize the dimensional structure based on Buckingham's π theorem and similarity principles (Akpakpan, 2018; Glaws, 2018; Shen & Lin, 2018; Shen, Lin, & Chang, 2018). Given the large complex domains of expression in big data, connected ensembles, and multitier functional form expressions had to be reflected within the data structures (Akpakpan, 2018; Deng, El Naqa, & Xing, 2019; Wu et al., 2019). The popularity of algorithms in the expression of complex domains was the result of the need for flexibility demanded at the data model level which multidimensional modeling does not allow (Elshawi, Sakr, Talia, & Trunfio, 2018; Ramírez-Gallego, Fernández, García, Chen, & Herrera, 2018). Unfortunately, without constraints, the algorithms produced solutions that were difficult to explain or useless for management decision support (Guidotti et al., 2018; Shah, 2018).

The proper structuring of the data models for management analytics and decision support required three critical changes to the data-modeling process: (a) learning the ontology of the subject of interest from the available data; (b) engineering the features needed within the data; and (c) applying analytic formulation techniques to evolve the data to the right grain for analysis process (Akpakpan, 2018; Bertossi & Milani, 2018). The solution architecture combined ontology learning, data engineering, and analytic formulation techniques to derive extensions to data models to improve management analytics and decision support in big data environment (Tremblay et al., 2017, Zojaji, & Ebadzadeh, 2016). In this context, ontology learning identifies the concepts within the available metadata and data set to construct the map of the business situation expressed; data engineering techniques connect the concepts to the available data; and analytic formulation techniques extend the data elements to analytic elements as semantic, symbolic, and dimensional forms demanded by the analytic scenario (Akpakpan, 2018; Debattista, Attard, & Brennan, 2018; Sajjad, Bajwa, & Kazmi, 2019; Rao, 2019).

The task of building processes that would answer complex questions based on the available data demanded the combination of these techniques to generate data models at the most appropriate level required for management problem-solving. Akpakpan (2018) demonstrated the technique on 15 TB database with 700 attributes from 137 datasets which had a total of 1.7 billion records representing transactions over three years from a medical supply company with an ill-defined growth and profitability problem. The process generated a comprehensive management plan to return to profitability and growth in 3 years through programs like (a) special pricing and product promotions with sales representative, (b) monitoring group pricing and rebating arrangement, (c) expanding onsite supply program to reduce member in group purchasing arrangements, (d) improving price blocking logic, and (e) establishing performance benchmarks for products manufactured. These programs tackled issues of customer churn, price leakage, customer value decay, sales representative gaming, and expensive internal manufacturing processes which were responsible for challenges with growth and profitability. The validity these programs were demonstrated through simulations, which confirmed the return to profitability in about 2.8 years. The company continues to use the algorithms designed with modification to manage profitability and growth to this day. The first implication of the demonstration was that management tasks modeled as complex dynamic constrained optimization and simulation problems can be solved to produce predictable results based on the parameters and boundaries established within the data, but the data must be big data. The second implication was that popular concepts in management research like the design of experiments and hypothesis-driven approach could no longer be considered superior to a hypothesis-free search, discovery, validation, deployment of logic to support management tasks as dictated by the applied sciences of management and decisions (Akpakpan, 2018).

The Impact on the Multigenerational Workforce

The cognitive paradigm of management demands an extreme emphasis on technological knowledge, and quantitative abilities, and less so on experience and intuition, which are eroding as determinants of competence (Briken, Chillas, Krzywdzinski, & Marks, 2017). Adapting to new tools, technologies, techniques, and practices are much more valuable in the modern workforce at all levels (Berg, Branka, & Kismihók, 2018). Using computers and mobile devices in the work of management, and understanding when analytics, algorithms, and automation are not performing as expected are also critical in this new digital workforce (Schwab, 2017). Because most of these requirements are relatively new to the business environment, they would tend to put the older worker at much of a disadvantage (Fisk, Czaja, Rogers, Charness, & Sharit, 2018; Neumark, Burn, & Button, 2019).

Studies that include examination of the *Unified Theory of Acceptance and Use of Technology* in many different contexts suggests significant disparities in technology literacy in multigenerational workforce (Chopdar, Korfiatis, Sivakumar, & Lytras, 2018; Magsamen-Conrad, Upadhyaya, Joa, & Dowd, 2015; Tams, & Dulipovici, 2019; Ratten, 2018). Perception is that cognitive capabilities parallel to technological literacy, given pronouncements like "young people are just smarter" [and] "people over 45 basically die in terms of new ideas" ascribed to Mark Zuckerberg of Facebook and Vinod Khosla of Sun Microsystems (now Oracle), respectively (Kopytoff, 2014). Despite these pronouncements, the older computer-savvy workers, managers, and executives were able to use their experience to effectively manage the delivery of analytic and cognitive products (Ratten, 2018). The challenge to overcome for the older worker or manager is the bias of ageism, considered discriminatory (Price, 2018).

Among each of the generations, the Silent and Baby Boomer generation workers held most of the executive and top management positions and were the leaders to advance the cognitive paradigm of management (Chopdar, Korfiatis, Sivakumar, & Lytras, 2018; Ratten, 2018). However, the tendency to defer to the technology managers and executives to provide strategic direction for delivery, which creates the information technology *blame game* when the organization loses competitive advantage, as noted with Sears, IBM, Dell, Xerox, Motorola, and other major brands that failed with data analytics and cognitive capabilities as strategic imperatives (Ansoff, Kipley, Lewis, Helm-Stevens, & Ansoff, 2019; Chopdar, Korfiatis, Sivakumar, & Lytras, 2018; Ratten, 2018).

The middle-aged (Generation X), and younger generations (Generations Y and Z) welcome and leverage the cognitive management transition as the ladder to the executive suite (Ansoff, Kipley, Lewis, Helm-Stevens, & Ansoff, 2019; Mol, & Birkinshaw, 2009). Generational diversity in the executive suite and top-management is an essential driver for the new business wave and transformations to automation, algorithms, and artificial intelligence augmentation of human capabilities for sustainable efficiency in managing businesses (Beneventi, 2018; Urick, 2019). The generational diversity provides the opportunity for the diffusion of business and technology innovation across workplace generational boundaries, and the recognition, for now, that age remains inseparable from credibility (Hewitt-Dundas, & Roper, 2018; Tams & Dulipovici, 2019; Ratten, 2018; Vasconcelos, 2018; Warhurst & Black, 2015).

Conclusion

This chapter covered a new paradigm of management, aptly termed, the cognitive paradigm of management. The cognitive paradigm of management evolved from the data analytics paradigm as a result of new challenges created by business complexity and big data. Specifically, the need to focus management practice on the transformation of big data to cognitive capabilities across the organization, through the interoperability of analytics, algorithms, automation, and artificial intelligence, in a digital workforce in support collaboration of man and machine assets. The cognitive paradigm of management promises to elevate human labor to the high-value tasks that machines are not capable of doing, advancing the digital business model by reducing transaction cost, expanding the operational scale, and value delivery to the end user. The cognitive management paradigm has enormous implications for all industries and workers. In healthcare, the cognitive approach promises a value-based care delivery system with the patient-provider interaction without constraints of third-party intermediaries like health insurance companies, benefit managers, and physician organizations, as all governance and approval needs would all be part of cognitive processes executing in the background (Pang, Yang, Khedri, & Zhang, 2018; Reichert, 2018). In financial services, the cognitive management approach is disrupting functions provided by service intermediaries enabling the direct interaction of the customer with the provider of the services needed (Melanie, Jason, Soichiro, Frank, & Paolo, 2019; van Rijmenam, 2019). In other industries, marketplaces will evolve where management tasks involved in the direct interaction of the service provider and the consumer of the service, are governed and verified by the parties involved (Melanie, Jason, Soichiro, Frank, & Paolo, 2019; Reichert, 2018). This future of management is the complete democratization of business efficiency, which entails the elimination of all pockets of inefficiencies, including the strategies to ensure that business knowledge and competence of the older generations (Silent and Baby Boomer generations) are leveraged to support innovation with technology made possible by the middle-aged and younger generations (Generations X, Y, and Z).

THOUGHTS FROM THE ACADEMIC ENTREPRENEUR

The problem to be solved:

• Establish a rationale for a new paradigm of management which leverages algorithms, automation, and artificial intelligence to extend organizational cognitive capabilities

The goals:

• Present two critical requirements of the cognitive paradigm of management: improved information processes for organizational cognitive enablement, and strategies for multigenerational diversification of executive and top-management ranks to accelerate the adoption of cognitive enablement as a strategic imperative.

The questions to ask:

• How can organizations improve the results of investments to achieve the cognitive enablement needed?

• How should organizations advance these cognitive enablement programs to achieve decentralized autonomous business entities profitably?

Today's Business Application:

• Essential data and analytics strategy that integrates ontology learning, data engineering, and analytic formulation techniques to create analytic extensions of data models in support of organizational cognitive enablement.

• Provide perspective for the redesign of business systems and processes to take advantage of the advances in analytics, algorithms, automation, and artificial intelligence.

• Provide awareness of market disruptions of digital business ecosystems and marketplaces powered by analytics, algorithms, automation and artificial intelligence, and the need for organizations to remake themselves to prevent loss of market share to competitors with the foresight to establish such eco-systems and markets.

REFERENCES

Akpakpan, N. (2018). *Analytic extensions to the data model for management analytics and decision support in the big data environment* (Doctoral dissertation). Available from ProQuest Dissertations and Theses database. (UMI No. 10840512)

Amankwah-Amoah, J., & Adomako, S. (2019). Big data analytics and business failures in data-rich environments: An organizing framework. *Computers in Industry, 105*, 204-212. doi:10.1016/j.compind.2018.12.015

Andraszewicz, S., Scheibehenne, B., Rieskamp, J., Grasman, R., Verhagen, J., & Wagenmakers, E. J. (2015). An introduction to Bayesian hypothesis testing for management research. *Journal of Management, 41*, 521-543. doi:10.1177/0149206314560412

Ansoff, H. I., Kipley, D., Lewis, A. O., Helm-Stevens, R., & Ansoff, R. (2019). Diagnosing future general management capability. In *Implanting Strategic Management* (pp. 105-125). Palgrave Macmillan: Cham, Switzerland. doi:10.1007/978-3-319-99599-1_8

Ariño, M. A., de Santiago, R., & Seager, P. H. (2017). Decision analysis: The "science" of predicting your next hit. In *Managing media businesses* (pp. 101-112). Palgrave Macmillan: Cham, Switzerland. doi:10.1007/978-3-319-52021-6_6

Atagün, A. O., Kamacı, H., & Oktay, O. (2018). Reduced soft matrices and generalized products with applications in decision-making. *Neural Computing and Applications, 29*, 445-456. doi:10.1007/s00521-016-2542-y

Ayoub, K., & Payne, K. (2016). Strategy in the age of artificial intelligence. *Journal of Strategic Studies, 39*, 793-819. doi:10.1080/01402390.2015.1088838

Bäck, T., Fogel, D. B., & Michalewicz, Z. (Eds.). (2018). *Evolutionary computation 1: Basic algorithms and operators*. Boca Raton, FL: CRC Press.

Baker, T. (2019). The dumbing down of work. In *Bringing the human being back to work* (pp. 3-11). Palgrave Macmillan, Cham, Switzerland. doi:10.1007/978-3-319-93172-2_1

Beneventi, P. (Ed.). (2018). *Technology and the new generation of active citizens: Emerging research and opportunities: Emerging research and opportunities*. Hersey, PA: IGI Global.

Bertossi, L., & Milani, M. (2018). Ontological multidimensional data models and contextual data quality. *Journal of Data and Information Quality (JDIQ), 9*(3), 14. doi:10.1145/3148239

Berg, A. M., Branka, J., & Kismihók, G. (2018). Combining learning analytics with job market intelligence to support learning at the workplace. In *Digital workplace learning* (pp. 129-148). Springe: Cham, Switzerland. doi:10.1007/978-3-319-46215-8_8

Boutkhoum, O., & Hanine, M. (2017, December). An integrated decision-making prototype based on OLAP systems and multicriteria analysis for complex decision-making problems. In *Applied informatics* (Vol. 4, No. 1, p. 11). Springer Open. doi:10.1186/s40535-017-0041-6

Bodroži, Z., & Adler, P. S. (2018). The evolution of management models: A neo-Schumpeterian theory. *Administrative Science Quarterly, 63*(1), 85-129. doi:10.1177/0001839217704811

Branke, J. (2016). MCDA and multi-objective evolutionary algorithms. In *Multiple criteria decision analysis* (pp. 977-1008). New York, NY: Springer. doi:10.1007/978-1-4939-3094-4_23

Briken, K., Chillas, S., Krzywdzinski, M., & Marks, A. (2017). Labor process theory and the new digital workplace. *The new digital workplace: How new technologies revolutionize work*. London, UK: Palgrave, Macmillan.

Burke, W. W. (2017). *Organization change: Theory and practice*. Thousand Oaks, CA: Sage Publications.

Caputo, F., Cillo, V., Candelo, E., & Liu, Y. (2019). Innovating through digital revolution: The role of soft skills and big data in increasing firm performance. *Management Decision*. doi:10.1108/MD-07-2018-0833

Camisón, C., & Villar-López, A. (2014). Organizational innovation as an enabler of technological innovation capabilities and firm performance. *Journal of Business Research, 67*, 2891-2902. doi:10.1016/j.jbusres.2012.06.004

Ceruzzi, P. E. (2003). *A history of modern computing*. Cambridge, MA: The MIT Press.

Chandra, P., & Gupta, M. K. (2018). Comprehensive survey on data warehousing research. *International Journal of Information Technology, 10*(2), 217-224. doi:10.1007/s41870-017-0067-y

Chang, A. B., Oppenheimer, J. J., Weinberger, M., Weir, K., Rubin, B. K., & Irwin, R. S. (2016). Use of management pathways or algorithms in children with chronic cough: systematic reviews. *Chest, 149*(1), 106-119. doi:10.1378/chest.15-1403

Chen, H., & Bai, Y. (2017, October). Innovation and reconstruction of management mode in internet era. In *2017 International Conference on Education Science and Economic Management (ICESEM 2017)*. Atlantis Press. doi:10.2991/icesem-17.2017.35

Chopdar, P. K., Korfiatis, N., Sivakumar, V. J., & Lytras, M. D. (2018). Mobile shopping apps adoption and perceived risks: A cross-country perspective utilizing the Unified Theory of Acceptance and Use of Technology. *Computers in Human Behavior, 86*, 109-128. doi:10.1016/j.chb.2018.04.017

Christidis, K., & Devetsikiotis, M. (2016). Blockchains and smart contracts for the internet of things. *IEEE Access, 4,* 2292-2303. doi:10.1109/ ACCESS.2016.2566339

Daft, R. L. (2015). *Organization theory and design.* Boston, MA: Cengage Learning.

Davis, R. (1958). A philosophy of management. *Academy of Management Journal, 1*(3), 37-40. doi:10.5465/254624

Debattista, J., Attard, J., & Brennan, R. (2018, August). Semantic data ingestion for intelligent, value-driven big data analytics. In *2018 4th International Conference on Big Data Innovations and Applications (Innovate-Data)* (pp. 1-8). doi:10.1109/Innovate-Data.2018.00008

Deng, J., El Naqa, I., & Xing, L. (Eds.). (2019). *Machine learning with radiation oncology big data.* Lausanne, Switzerland: Frontiers Media SA. doi:10.3389/978-2-88945-730-4

Donaldson, G. A. (2016). *When America liked Ike: How moderates won the 1952 presidential election and reshaped American politics.* Washington DC: Rowman & Littlefield Publishers.

Elshawi, R., Sakr, S., Talia, D., & Trunfio, P. (2018). Big data systems meet machine learning challenges: Towards big data science as a service. *Big Data Research, 14,* 1-11. doi:10.1016/j.bdr.2018.04.004

Eroshkin, S. Y., Koryagin, N. D., Kovkov, D. V., Panov, D. V., & Sukhorukov, A. I. (2017). The paradigm of the integration of different types of management information systems in investment and construction company implementing the project approach. *Procedia Computer Science, 103,* 605-608. doi:10.1016/j. procs.2017.01.076

Frank, M., Roehrig, P., & Pring, B. (2017). *What to do when machines do everything: How to get ahead in a world of AI, algorithms, bots, and big data.* Hoboken, NJ: Wiley & Sons.

Fisk, A. D., Czaja, S. J., Rogers, W. A., Charness, N., & Sharit, J. (2018). *Designing for older adults: Principles and creative human factors approaches.* Boca Raton, FL: CRC Press.

Fu, T. (2018). What algorithms want imagination in the age of computing. *Journal of Information, Communication & Society, 21,* 1849-1851. doi:10.1080/136 9118X.2017.1409785

Gartner, Inc. (2016). *Predicts 2014: Business intelligence and analytics will remain CIO's top technology priority.* Retrieved from http://www.gartner.com/

George, G., Osinga, E. C., Lavie, D., & Scott, B. A. (2016). Big data and data science methods for management research. *Academy of Management Journal, 59,* 1493-1507. doi:10.5465/amj.2016.4005

Geyer-Klingeberg, J., Nakladal, J., Baldauf, F., & Veit, F. (2018). Process mining and robotic process automation: A perfect match. *Proceedings of the Dissertation*

Award, Demonstration, and Industrial Track at BPM, 9-14. Retrieved from https://bpm2017.cs.upc.edu/

Glaws, A. T. (2018). *Parameter dimension reduction for scientific computing* (Doctoral dissertation). Available from ProQuest Dissertations and Theses database. (UMI No. 10980910)

Grover, V., Chiang, R. H., Liang, T. P., & Zhang, D. (2018). Creating strategic business value from big data analytics: A research framework. *Journal of Management Information Systems*, *35*, 388-423. doi:10.1080/07421222.2018.1451951

Guidotti, R., Monreale, A., Ruggieri, S., Turini, F., Giannotti, F., & Pedreschi, D. (2018). A survey of methods for explaining black box models. *ACM cCmputing Surveys (CSUR)*, *51*(5), 93. doi:10.1145/3236009

Harvey, H. B., & Sotardi, S. T. (2018). Key performance indicators and the balanced scorecard. *Journal of the American College of Radiology*, *15*, 1000-1001. doi:10.1016/j.jacr.2018.04.006

Haupt, G. (2018). Hierarchical thinking: a cognitive tool for guiding coherent decision-making in design problem-solving. *International Journal of Technology and Design Education*, *28*(1), 207-237. doi:10.1007/s10798-016-9381-0

Hazen, B. T., Skipper, J. B., Boone, C. A., & Hill, R. R. (2018). Back in business: Operations research in support of big data analytics for operations and supply chain management. *Annals of Operations Research*, *270*(1-2), 201-211. doi:10.1007/s10479-016-2226-0

Hewage, T. N., Halgamuge, M. N., Syed, A., & Ekici, G. (2018). Big data techniques of Google, Amazon, Facebook, and Twitter. *Journal of Communications*, *13*(2). doi:10.12720/jcm.13.2.94-100

Hewitt-Dundas, N., & Roper, S. (2018). Exploring market failures in open innovation. *International Small Business Journal*, *36*(1), 23-40. doi:10.1177/0266242617696347

Ingvaldsen, J. A. (2015). Organizational learning: Bringing the forces of production back in. *Organization Studies*, *36*, 423–444. doi:10.1177/0170840614561567

Irene, B., Marika, A., Giovanni, A., & Mario, C. (2016). Indicators and metrics for social business: a review of current approaches. *Journal of Social Entrepreneurship*, *7*(1), 1-24. doi:10.1080/19420676.2015.1049286

Kanter, J. M., & Veeramachaneni, K. (2015, October). Deep feature synthesis: Towards automating data science endeavors. In *2015 IEEE International Conference on Data Science and Advanced Analytics (DSAA)* (pp. 1-10). IEEE. doi:10.1109/DSAA.2015.7344858

Kasemsap, K. (2018). Mastering business process management and business intelligence in global business. In *Global Business Expansion: Concepts, Methodologies, Tools, and Applications* (pp. 76-96). doi:10.4018/978-1-5225-5481-3.ch006

Kassarnig, V., & Wotawa, F. (2018a). An approach to automatically extract predictive properties from nominal attributes in relational databases. In *2018 IEEE International Conference on Big Data (Big Data)* (pp. 4932-4939). doi:10.1109/BigData.2018.8622359

Kassarnig, V., & Wotawa, F. (2018b). Evolutionary propositionalization of multi-relational data. *International Journal of Software Engineering and Knowledge Engineering, 28*, 1739-1754. doi:10.1142/S0218194018400260

Kimball, R., Ross, M., Thornthwaite, W., Mundy, J., & Becker, B. (2008).*The data warehouse lifecycle toolkit*. Indianapolis, IN: Wiley & Sons.

Kleindorfer, P. R., Kunreuther, H., Kunreuther, H. G., & Schoemaker, P. J. (1993). *Decision sciences: An integrative perspective*. Cambridge, United Kingdom: Cambridge University Press.

Kochan, T. A., Riordan, C. A., Kowalski, A. M., Khan, M., & Yang, D. (2019). The changing nature of employee and labor-management relationships. *Annual Review of Organizational Psychology and Organizational Behavior, 6*, 195-219. doi:10.1146/annurev-orgpsych-012218-015335

Kopytoff, V. (2014). Tech industry job ads: Older workers need not apply. *Fortune. 2014*. Retrieved from: http://fortune.com/2014/06/19/tech-job-ads-discrimination/

Koumparoulis, D. N., & Vlachopoulioti, A. (2012). One hundred years of Taylorism: is it still relevant today?. *Academic Research International, 3*, 420. Retrieved from http://www.journals.savap.org.pk/

Kumar, A., McCann, R., Naughton, J., & Patel, J. M. (2016). Model selection management systems: The next frontier of advanced analytics. *ACM SIGMOD Record, 44*(4), 17-22. doi:10.1145/2935694.2935698

Lacity, M., & Willcocks, L. P. (2018). *Robotic process and cognitive automation: the next phase*. Ashford, UK: SB Publishing.

Legner, C., Eymann, T., Hess, T., Matt, C., Böhmann, T., Drews, P., . . . & Ahlemann, F. (2017). Digitalization: Opportunity and challenge for the business and information systems engineering community. *Business & Information Systems Engineering, 59*, 301-308. doi:10.1007/s12599-017-0484-2

Le Masson, P., Dorst, K., & Subrahmanian, E. (2013). Design theory: History, state of the art, and advancements. *Research Engineering Design, 24*, 97–103. doi:10.1007/s00163-013-0154-4

Leonardi, P., Levina, N., Truelove, E., & Vaast, E. (2018, July). How advances in digital technologies reconfigure organizational Coordination processes. In *Academy of Management Proceedings* (Vol. 2018, No. 1, p. 14831). Briarcliff Manor, NY: Academy of Management. doi:10.5465/AMBPP.2018.14831symposium

Ma, W., Jiang, Y., Liu, W., Luo, X., & McAreavey, K. (2018, April). Expected utility with relative loss reduction: A unifying decision model for resolving four well-known paradoxes. In *Thirty-Second AAAI Conference on Artificial Intelligence*.

Magsamen-Conrad, K., Upadhyaya, S., Joa, C. Y., & Dowd, J. (2015). Bridging the divide: Using UTAUT to predict multigenerational tablet adoption practices. *Computers in Human Behavior, 50*, 186-196. doi:10.1016/j.chb.2015.03.032

Martínez, L., Rodriguez, R. M., & Herrera, F. (2015). Dealing with hesitant fuzzy linguistic information in decision making. In *The 2-tuple Linguistic Model* (pp. 113-129). Springer, Cham, Switzerland. doi:10.1007/978-3-319-24714-4_6

Melanie, S., Jason, P., Soichiro, T., Frank, W., & Paolo, T. (Eds.). (2019). *Blockchain economics: Implications of distributed ledgers-markets, communications networks, and algorithmic reality* (Vol. 1).Hackensack, NJ: World Scientific.

Mendling, J., Decker, G., Richard, H., Hajo, A., & Ingo, W. (2018). How do machine learning, robotic process automation, and blockchains affect the human factor in business process management? *Communications of the Association for Information Systems, 43*(Art. 19), 297-320. doi:10.17705/1CAIS.043XX

Mohanty, S., Jagadeesh, M., & Srivatsa, H. (2013). *Big data imperatives: Enterprise big data warehouse, BI implementations and analytics*. New York, NY: Apress.

Mol, M. J., & Birkinshaw, J. (2009). The sources of management innovation: When firms introduce new management practices. *Journal of Business Research, 62*, 1269-1280. doi:10.1016/j.jbusres.2009.01.001

Mortenson, M. J., Doherty, N. F., & Robinson, S. (2015). Operational research from Taylorism to Terabytes: A research agenda for the analytics age. *European Journal of Operational Research, 241*, 583-595. doi:10.1016/j.ejor.2014.08.029

Moukhi, N. E., Azami, I. E., & Mouloudi, A. (2018). Towards a new method for designing multidimensional models. *International Journal of Business Information Systems, 28*(1), 18-41. doi:10.1504/IJBIS.2018.091161

Neumark, D., Burn, I., & Button, P. (2019). Is it harder for older workers to find jobs? New and improved evidence from a field experiment. *Journal of Political Economy, 127*(2), 000-000. doi:10.1086/701029

Nissen, V. (2018). Applications of evolutionary algorithms to management problems. In *Innovative research methodologies in management* (pp. 211-235). Palgrave Macmillan, Cham, Switzerland. doi:10.1007/978-3-319-64394-6_9

Ormerod, R. (1999). Blackett the father of OR. *OR Insight, 12*(2), 14-20. doi:10.1057/ori.1999.8

Pang, Z., Yang, G., Khedri, R., & Zhang, Y. T. (2018). Introduction to the special section: convergence of automation technology, biomedical engineering, and health informatics toward the healthcare 4.0. *IEEE Reviews in Biomedical Engineering, 11*, 249-259. doi:10.1109/RBME.2018.2848518

Paudyal, P., & William Wong, B. L. (2018, September). Algorithmic opacity: making algorithmic processes transparent through abstraction hierarchy. In *Proceedings of the Human Factors and Ergonomics Society Annual*

Meeting (Vol. 62, No. 1, pp. 192-196). Los Angeles, CA: SAGE Publications. doi:10.1177/1541931218621046

Park, H. H., & Faerman, S. (2019). Becoming a manager: learning the importance of emotional and social competence in managerial transitions. *The American Review of Public Administration, 49*(1), 98-115. doi:10.1177/0275074018785448

Pedreschi, D., Giannotti, F., Guidotti, R., Monreale, A., Ruggieri, S., & Turini, F. (2019). *Meaningful Explanations of Black Box AI Decision Systems.* AAAI. Retrieved from https://www.aaai.org

Peng, G. (2017). Do computer skills affect worker employment?: An empirical study from CPS surveys. *Computers in Human Behavior, 74*, 26-34. doi:10.1016/j.chb.2017.04.013

Piaskowska, D., Nadolska, A., & Barkema, H. G. (2017). Embracing complexity: Learning from minority, 50-50, and majority joint venture experience. *Long Range Planning.* doi:10.1016/j.lrp.2017.10.001

Piciocchi, P., Bassano, C., Pietronudo, M. C., & Spohrer, J. C. (2019). Digital workers in service systems: Challenges and opportunities. In *Handbook of service science, Volume II* (pp. 409-432). Cham, Switzerland: SAGE Publications:

Price, L. (2018). *Managing the four different generations in the workplace effectively, efficiently, and successfully.* Meadville, PA: Fulton Books.

Rahman, N., & Rutz, D. (2019). Building data warehouses using automation. In *Rapid automation: Concepts, methodologies, tools, and applications* (pp. 735-759). Hersey, PA: IGI Global.

Ramírez-Gallego, S., Fernández, A., García, S., Chen, M., & Herrera, F. (2018). Big data: Tutorial and guidelines on information and process fusion for analytics algorithms with MapReduce. *Information Fusion, 42*, 51-61. doi:10.1016/j.inffus.2017.10.001

Rao, A. P. (2019). Discovering knowledge hidden in big data from machine-learning techniques. In *Web services: Concepts, methodologies, tools, and applications* (pp. 684-700). Hershey, PA: IGI Global.

Ratten, V. (2018). Older entrepreneurship: A literature review and research agenda. *Journal of Enterprising Communities: People and Places in the Global Economy.* doi:10.1108/JEC-08-2018-0054

Reichert, M. (2018). Enabling flexible and robust business process automation for the agile enterprise. In *The essence of software engineering* (pp. 203-220). Springer, Cham, Switzerland. doi:10.1007/978-3-319-73897-0

Rosiak, T., & Postula, A. (2018). Competitive advantages in millennials' reality. *Economic and Social Development: Book of Proceedings*, 468-475.

Russell, S., Hauert, S., Altman, R., & Veloso, M. (2015). Ethics of artificial intelligence. *Nature, 521*, 415-416. Retrieved from http://faculty.engineering.asu.edu/

Ross, J. E. (1976). *Modern management and information systems.* Reston, VA: Reston Publishing Company.

Sajjad, R., Bajwa, I. S., & Kazmi, R. (2019). Handling semantic complexity of big data using machine learning and RDF ontology model. *Symmetry, 11,* 309. doi:10.3390/sym11030309

Schwab, K. (2017). *The fourth industrial revolution.* New York, NY: Crown Publishing Group.

Sengupta, R. N., Gupta, A., & Dutta, J. (Eds.). (2016). *Decision sciences: theory and practice.* Boca Raton, FL: CRC Press.

Schildt, H. (2017). Big data and organizational design–the brave new world of algorithmic management and computer augmented transparency. *Innovation, 19*(1), 23-30. doi:10.1080/14479338.2016.1252043

Shah, H. (2018). Algorithmic accountability. *Philosophical Transactions of the Royal Society A: Mathematical, Physical and Engineering Sciences, 376*(2128), 20170362. doi:10.1098/rsta.2017.0362

Shen, W., & Lin, D. K. (2018). A conjugate model for dimensional analysis. *Technometrics, 60*(1), 79-89. doi:10.1080/00401706.2017.1291451

Shen, W., Lin, D. K., & Chang, C. J. (2018). Design and analysis of computer experiment via dimensional analysis. *Quality Engineering, 30,* 311-328. doi:10.1 080/08982112.2017.1320726

Shermin, V. (2017). Disrupting governance with blockchains and smart contracts. *Strategic Change, 26,* 499-509. doi:10.1002/jsc.2150

Shiau, W. L., Chen, S. Y., & Tsai, Y. C. (2015). Management information systems issues: co-citation analysis of journal articles. *International Journal of Electronic Commerce Studies, 6*(1), 145-162. doi:10.7903/ijecs.1393

Smith, V. L., & Wilson, B. J. (2019). *Humanomics: Moral sentiments and the Wealth of Nations for the Twenty-First Century.* United Kingdom: Cambridge University Press. doi:10.1017/9781108185561

Stewart, M. (2006). The management myth. *Atlantic Monthly, 297*(5), 80.

Sułkowski, Ł., & Kaczorowska-Spychalska, D. (2018, July). Internet of things-new paradigm of learning: Challenges for business. In *International Conference on Applied Human Factors and Ergonomics* (pp. 307-318). Springer, Cham, Switzerland. doi:10.1007/978-3-319-94866-9_31

Swan, M. (2018). Blockchain for business: Next-generation enterprise artificial intelligence systems. In *Advances in Computers* (Vol. 111, pp. 121-162). doi:10.1016/bs.adcom.2018.03.013

Swan, M. (2015, March). Blockchain thinking: The brain as a DAC (decentralized autonomous organization). In *Texas Bitcoin Conference* (pp. 27-29). doi:10.1109/MTS.2015.2494358

Tams, S., & Dulipovici, A. M. (2019, January). The creativity model of age and innovation with IT: How to counteract the effects of age stereotyping on user innovation. In *Proceedings of the 52nd Hawaii International Conference on System Sciences.* doi:10125/60089

Tapscott, D., & Tapscott, A. (2016). *Blockchain revolution: how the technology behind bitcoin is changing money, business, and the world.* New York, NY: Penguin. doi:10.1016/j.apergo.2016.07.009

Tekez, E. K. (2018). Development of an expert system for demand management process. *International Journal of Computer Integrated Manufacturing, 31,* 970-977. doi:10.1080/0951192X.2018.1481297

Thomas, I. (2016). Putting big data at the heart of the decision-making process. In *Big data and business analytics* (pp. 174-191). Boca Raton, FL: Auerbach Publications.

Tremblay, S., Gagnon, J. F., Lafond, D., Hodgetts, H. M., Doiron, M., & Jeuniaux, P. P. (2017). A cognitive prosthesis for complex decision-making. *Applied Ergonomics, 58,* 349-360.

Tsoukas, H. (2017). Don't simplify, complexify: From disjunctive to conjunctive theorizing in organization and management studies. *Journal of Management Studies, 54*(2), 132-153. doi:10.1111/joms.12219

Turban, E. (1993). *Decision support and expert systems: management support systems.* Upper Saddle River, NJ: Prentice Hall PTR.

Urick, M. J. (2019). *The generation myth: How to improve intergenerational relationships in the workplace.* New York, NY: Business Expert Press:

van Rijmenam, M. (2019). *Organization of tomorrow: How AI, blockchain, and analytics Turn your business into a data organization.* London, United Kingdom: Routledge.

Vasconcelos, A. F. (2018). Older workers as a source of wisdom capital: broadening perspectives. *Revista de Gestão, 25*(1), 102-118. doi:10.1108/REGE-11-2017-002

Veit, F., Geyer-Klingeberg, J., Madrzak, J., Haug, M., & Thomson, J. (2017, September). The proactive insights engine: Process mining meets machine learning and artificial intelligence. In *BPM (Demos).* Retrieved from https://bpm2017.cs.upc.edu/

Von den Eichen, S. F., Matzler, K., & Hautz, J. (2019). Open management as management innovation: Thoughts about new business and disruption in consulting. In *Advances in consulting research* (pp. 213-227). Springer, Cham, Switzerland. doi:10.1007/978-3-319-95999-3_10

Voithofer, R., & Ham, M. (2018). Ethical issues and potential unintended consequences of data-based decision making. *Responsible Analytics and Data Mining in Education: Global Perspectives on Quality, Support, and Decision-Making, 55.*

Warhurst, R. P., & Black, K. E. (2015). It's never too late to learn. *Journal of Workplace Learning, 27*, 457-472. doi:10.1108/JWL-07-2014-0050

Wang, M., & Wang, H. (2006). From process logic to business logic: A cognitive approach to business process management. *Information & Management, 43*(2), 179-193. doi:10.1016/j.im.2005.06.001.

Wang, P., Chaudhry, S., & Da Xu, L. (2016). Introduction: Advances in e-business engineering and management. *Information Technology Management, 17*(3), 199-201. doi:10.1007/s10799-016-0260-x

Williams, S. (2016). *Business intelligence strategy and big data analytics: A general management perspective.* Cambridge, MA: Morgan Kaufmann.

Witten, I. H., Frank, E., Hall, M. A., & Pal, C. J. (2016). *Data Mining: Practical machine learning tools and techniques.* Morgan Kaufmann: Cambridge, MA: Morgan Kaufmann.

Wu, C., Zhou, F., Ren, J., Li, X., Jiang, Y., & Ma, S. (2019). A selective review of multi-level omics data integration using variable selection. *High-Throughput, 8*(1), 4. doi:10.3390/ht8010004

Xing, B., & Marwala, T. (2018). *The synergy of blockchain and artificial intelligence.* doi:10.2139/ssrn.3225357

Yermack, D. (2017). Corporate governance and blockchains. *Review of Finance, 21*(1), 7-31. doi:10.1093/rof/rfw074

Zojaji, Z., & Ebadzadeh, M. M. (2016). Semantic schema theory for genetic programming. *Applied Intelligence, 44*(1), 67-87. doi:10.1007/s10489-015-0696-4

About the Author

Dr. Nsikak Akpakpan resides in the historic town of Elmhurst in Illinois. Dr. Nsikak is a Senior Principal of Technology Innovation in Health Industries at Clarity Insights, a Chicago based pure-play data analytics consulting company. Nsikak has 20 years' experience in defining business, technology, information, and organizational strategy within Health Industries. He focuses on using data to drive analytics strategy & execution, algorithm development, intelligent automation, artificial intelligence, and new digital business delivery models to create value for healthcare providers, payers, patients and supplier partners.

Dr. Nsikak holds a Ph.D. in Applied Management and Decision Sciences from Walden University, a Master of Business Administration in Information and Decision Sciences and Management Information Systems from University of Illinois at Chicago, Master of Public Health in Health Resources Management, Computational Epidemiology and Biostatistics from the University of Illinois at Chicago. He also holds a post-graduate Diploma in Anesthesiology (DA) from University of Calabar Teaching Hospital, Nigeria and Royal London Hospital Department of Anesthesiology as well as Bachelor of Medicine and Bachelor of Surgery (M.B., B.S) from University of Nigeria.

To reach Dr. Nsikak Akpakpan for additional information, please **email:** nakpakpan1@gmail.com

Multigenerational Leadership and Engagement: A Balancing Act for 21st Century Leaders

Dr. Gail Ade, Dr. Tokunbo Majaro, & Dr. Marietta Poshi

Today's workforce is uniquely more diverse than ever; managing employees from several generations is a 21st-century leadership and business reality (Arsenault, 2004). As of 2019, the current U.S. workforce encompasses diverse employees with 0-55 formative years of professional experience working side-by-side to achieve a common vision. The dynamic economic climate, extended life expectancy, delayed retirement, secondary careers, and desire to remain active are some of the reasons for multiple generations in the workplace (Clark, 2017; Domeyer, 2006; Fitch & Van Brunt, 2016). According to the Pew Research Center (2019), the five existing generations in the workforce are the Silent Generation (1928-1945), Baby Boomers (1946–1964), Generation X (1965–1980), Generation Y or Millennials (1981–1996) and Generation Z (1997–Present). These generations vastly differ in characteristics, lifestyles, values, and attitudes due to many phenomena, such as globalization, scientific progress, politics, social change, and technological advancements (Williams & Page, 2011). Unquestionably, these differences present unique opportunities and challenges for 21st-century leaders across all industries. Consequently, leading multiple generations is a balancing act for leaders to adequately accommodate intergenerational attributes, maximize potentials, and integrate the influence of cross-generations (Kruse,

2015; Savino, 2017). Therefore, leaders must exercise refractive thinking to meaningfully engage employees and maximize the immense intellectual capital that generational diversity offers.

U.S. Workforce: Generations and Characteristics

Multigenerational workforce provides an opportunity for leaders to utilize the various distinctive strengths that each generation offers. Leveraging the aptitudes of all generational cohorts requires a deep conversance of the characteristics of each generation, as well as differences, similarities, expectations, and motivators (Kruse, 2015). Understanding these generational differences raises leadership awareness that one size does not fit all, especially given the apparent disparities in characteristics and motivators.

Silent Generations or Traditionalist

Silent generation (1928–1945), also known as Traditionalist, witnessed the Great Depression and World War II (Clark, 2017). Due to these historical events, the Traditionalists have a strong sense of patriotism, morality, and civic duty (Clark, 2017). Although the Traditionalists are approximately 3% of the current workforce, they are hardworking employees who respect authority, value structure and exude strong work ethics (Dakodia, Rai, & Chawla, 2015). Traditionalists favor a clear directive style of command-and-control often through formal channels (Salahuddin, 2010). One way to motivate Traditionalists is to maximize their wealth of experience and value their input in the decision-making process (Al-Asfour & Lettau, 2014; Bursch & Kelly, 2014). To effectively engage Traditionalist, leaders must demonstrate compassion, understanding, and create a positive working relationship through trust and respect (Society for Human Resource Management [SHRM], 2004).

Baby Boomers

Baby Boomers (1944–1964) lived through the Cold War, Vietnam War, and revolution (Sahraee & Abdullah, 2017; Wiedmer, 2015). Baby Boomers were loyal and conscientious workers who earned college degrees to gain upward mobility and stability in their careers (Wiedmer, 2015). The careers of Baby Boomers offered novel identities, but also challenged work-life balance (Levenberg, & Aaron, 2018). Success, recognition, and opportunities inspire Baby Boomers to expand professional reach (Fishman, 2016). To engage the Baby Boomers, leaders should show appreciation, support a work/life balance structure, and involve them in the decision-making and implementation stages of change initiatives (SHRM, 2004). Furthermore, Baby Boomers are not technologically savvy, therefore would benefit from reverse mentoring (Al-Asfour & Lettau, 2014).

Generation X

Generation X (1965–1980) experienced an economic recession, high unemployment, and fiscal instabilities, which in turn, shaped their perspectives and professional outlook (Lee, Kippenbrock, & Emory, 2019). As a result, Generation X values independence, freedom and continual growth, but abhors rigid work environment and domineering authority (Lee et al., 2019). Generation X also values work/life balance and are willing to prioritize family over work (Levenberg, & Aaron, 2018). To engage Generation X, leaders must create a workplace that is less hierarchical and more socially interactive (Benson & Brown, 2011). Additionally, leaders must develop paths for career growth, learning opportunities, as well as guidelines (American Institute of Architects, 2006; SHRM, 2004).

Generation Y

Generation Y (1981-1996), also known as Millennials, experienced technological advancement and constant change in the business environment (Lee et al., 2019). Differing from Generation X, Millennials enjoyed a booming economy, therefore, are optimistic, confident, and team-oriented (Levenberg, & Aaron, 2018; Lee et al., 2019). Furthermore, Millennials are tech-savvy, multi-taskers, and flexible employees who value structure and order in the workplace (Gutierrez & Klein, 2017). Millennials use learning and development as a motivation for success (Naim & Lenkla, 2016). According to the U.S. Department of Commerce (2011), leaders should use an information communication style that highlights positive attributes to provide feedback regularly. Moreover, leaders must be honest, flexible, ethical and socially responsible (Heinzerling, 2018).

Generation Z

Generation Z (1997-present) is the most recent generation to enter the workforce (Williams, 2015). As a result of readily available technology, Generation Z are more technologically proficient, communicate differently, and habitually utilize smartphones and Internet (Shatto, 2017). Generation Z are pragmatic risk-takers who value appreciation for their multitasking and adaptive abilities (Wiedmer, 2015). Accomplishment and autonomy motivate Generation Z to take an entrepreneurial approach in careers and professional objectives. Generation Z also embraces diversity, inclusivity, open-mindedness and progressive equality (Nichols & Wright, 2018). Generation Z currently constitutes a small percentage of the workforce but are likely to be the majority over the next two decades. The preferred leadership style for Generation Z is conceivably similar to Generation Y (Al-Asfour & Lettau, 2014).

Multigenerational Engagement

Despite nuances and differences, each generation has strategic skillsets and critical job knowledge that are central determinants of organizational success. Accordingly, scholars and OD practitioners continue to show keen interest in understanding and meaningfully engaging employees from all walks of life. As a result, organizations consider employee engagement a business priority to achieve sustainable growth and competitive advantage. Anitha (2014) defined employee engagement as the innate willingness and commitment to contribute to organizational success passionately. Authentic engagement is the level of commitment and positive emotional attachment that employees have towards organizational values, i.e., the willingness to contribute to organizational success (Osborne & Hammoud, 2017). Employee engagement is the heightened level of passion that employees have towards their work, their commitment to the organization and the discretionary efforts that they put towards task completion. Employee engagement makes a big difference between wanting to be on the job and having to be there (Anitha, 2014).

Multigenerational employee engagement is a multifaceted psychosomatic premise that directly impacts corporate bottom-line and long-term sustainability. A research study by Gallup revealed that organizations with highly engaged employees outperform the competition by 147 % in earnings per share and 90 % advancement trend (PR Newswire, 2019). Productivity, efficacy, customer satisfaction, and retention also corresponds to the level of employee engagement (Andre, 2018; PR Newswire, 2019). Similarly, employee engagement inspires creativity and innovation in the workplace (Gichohi, 2014). For example, engaged employees embrace company culture and transcend self-interest for organizational vision (Anitha, 2014); engaged employees also welcome additional responsibilities and are willing to go the extra mile

(Gichohi, 2014). Besides, employee engagement is also a requisite for employee satisfaction. Satisfied employees offer unrivaled customer service, which in turn, increases customer loyalty and retention rates (Mone & London, 2018).

Inclusion. Researchers affirm inclusion as the pillar of employee engagement; without inclusion, there is no engagement. Inclusion is the psychological empowerment of employees in ways that allows meaningful contribution (McManus Warnell, 2015). Inclusion simplified is about valuing employees, while engagement embodies involving employees strategically. Inclusion involves sharing, acknowledging and rewarding both similarities and uniqueness (Buengeler, Leroy, & De-Stobbeleir, 2018). For multigenerational workforce, inclusion entails more than just valuing individuals from different generational cohorts. Dynamic inclusion encompasses motivating and sustaining individuals with different perspectives, preferences, and ideological expectations through acceptance, recognition, and appreciation (Buengeler, Leroy, & De-Stobbeleir, 2018; McManus Warnell, 2015). With a comprehensive approach to strategic modalities, an inclusive work environment can become a purposeful engagement manifesto for employees across different generations.

a. *Meaningful Work:* Organizational vision is the rallying point for employees to find their unique contribution (Loerzel, 2019). Thus, leaders must ensure that employees have a clear understanding of how their contribution enriches the overall mission of the company (Loerzel, 2019).

b. *Rewards & Recognition:* To incentivize and foster meaningful engagement, it is imperative to understand that one size does not fit all when it comes to bonuses and support. Beyond attractive and comparative benefits, leaders should recognize and celebrate exemplary performances through comprehensive reward schemes (Goldsmith, Greenberg, Robertson, & Hu-Chan,

2003). Benefit packages and rewards should be customizable and tailored broadly enough to appeal to different generations (Gladwell, Dorwart, Stone, & Hammond, 2010).

c. *Flexible Schedule:* To enhance mobility, freedom, and autonomy, leaders should create a friendly work environment with multiple communication channels and flexible schedules (Loerzel, 2019; Savino, 2017).

d. *Timely Feedback:* Feedback should be apt and tied to performance evaluation to reinforce positive accomplishments and motivate further improvements (Loerzel, 2019).

e. *Continuous Development:* Through formal and informal training, leaders can foster advancement, empowerment, innovation, and better performance (McManus Warnell, 2015).

Individuality. Another embodiment of inclusion keeping sight of individual employees because each generational cohort is a group of people molded into a coherent constituency (Neville, 2018). According to Bonfante (2015), leaders must not squeeze every generation into a box of conformity; instead, employees should be allowed to express themselves uniquely, so they can feel valued and embraced.

a. *Expression.* To tap into, inspire, and retain the unique creativity of the existing talent pool, effective leaders should allow individualistic expression in leveraging the capabilities of cross-generational employees (Whittenburg & Rogers, 2018).

b. *Openness.* Unlike conventional leaders, inclusive leaders listen and welcome diverse perspectives while motivating employees to maximize optimal results (Goldsmith et al., 2003). Being open to input from all employees, regardless of generation, also creates an avenue for free sharing of ideas and profound innovation (Goldsmith et al., 2003).

Mentorship. An engaging and inclusive work environment nurtures careers and empowers mentoring relationships between employees of different generations as a preemptive gateway for knowledge transfer and continuous development (Andre, 2018; Desai, Rao, & Jabeen, 2018). Akin to multidisciplinary teams, cross-generational mentoring creates a discourse space to develop an understanding of generational differences while facilitating productive learning and better working alliances (Andre, 2018). Although mentorship conventionally involved older employees mentoring younger hires, leaders may find it more productive to embrace reciprocal mentoring (also called reverse mentoring or mentoring up). Reciprocal mentoring creates a mutual exchange of knowledge, where older generations participate in mentoring to gain more understanding of the use of advanced technology, innovative trends, social media, digital world (Desai et al., 2018). Whereas, younger employees gain invaluable knowledge, training, and the support necessary for professional advancement and broader opportunities (Desai et al., 2018).

Multigenerational Leadership Strategies

As the driving force for all organizational goals, missions, and outcomes, leaders play a very crucial role in employee engagement and inclusion process. Successfully engaging a cross-generational workforce necessitates effective leaders who will incorporate the ideas and skills of newer generations and sustain the continued presence and value of seasoned employees (Al-Asfour & Lettau, 2014). Furthermore, leaders are also responsible for minimizing contentions and creating innovative ways to maximize intergenerational advantage (Casad & Bryant, 2016). Below are critical leadership strategies for multigenerational employee engagement:

Flexibility and adaptability. Flexible and adaptive leaders are pivotal to the profitability and long-term success of multigenerational workplaces (Osborne & Hammoud, 2017). The heterogeneous nature of the 21st-century workforce compels leaders to balance various leadership abilities, styles, and strategies to serve all stakeholders (Arsenault, 2004). For successful leaders, flexibility is vital not only to meet the unique needs of each generation, but also to motivate and recognize individual accomplishments (Goldsmith et al., 2003). Likewise, tactical adaptability is necessary for responding quickly to the ever-changing multicomplex internal and external contingencies. As daunting as it sounds, multiple stakeholders necessitates flexibility, open-mindedness, adaptive nature, quick response, and proactive measures (Batool, 2013). Irrefutably, no individual model of leadership or strategy is comprehensive enough to fully maximize the combination of talents, values, and ideologies that generational diversity offers.

Excellent communication. A distinctive competency for multigenerational leaders and employee engagement is explicit and ongoing communication (McManus Warnell, 2015; Osborne & Hammoud, 2017). The leadership ability to effectively communicate is the foundation for employee engagement (Osborne & Hammoud, 2017). Without the ability to communicate organizational objectives, leaders cannot create positive work relationships, shared or understood responsibilities, accountability, meaningful work, or impact corporate vision (Johnson, 2015). Correspondingly, an inclusive and engaging environment sets the tone for leadership practices when it comes to both expressive and receptive communication. Successful leaders do not just communicate; instead, they rely on strategic conversations to break down barriers among different generations (Brandts, Cooper, & Weber, 2014). When communicating, leaders must ensure the equitable and respectful treatment of all, irrespective of age (Johnson, 2015). Through effective communication, leaders can also build bonds, trust, and connections with their followers, a requisite for higher profitability and long-term success (Osborne & Hammoud, 2017).

Collaboration & team building. Workgroups are imperative to leverage organizational competitive advantage, which is why team building is a vital part of cross-generational leadership strategies. Without highly functioning and effectively interactive teams, no organization can readily adapt to the fluidity of the current business environment (Neville, 2018). Practical ways of ensuring better employee engagement include embodying the importance of teamwork via openness to new ideas and the willingness to integrate different perspectives into productive solutions (Bagshaw, Lepp & Zorn, 2007). Bagshaw et al, further recommended that generational team building starts with valuing the diversity of team members, open and participative communication, collaborative dialogue, building trust plus maintaining productive group interaction. Collaboration and team building are sustainable through clarity of responsibilities, ethical decision-making, effectual escalation and conflict resolution (Neville, 2018).

Conflict management. When people with distinct worldviews, values, and ideas work together side-by-side, conflict and challenges are inevitable. Thus, multigenerational leaders must facilitate collaboration and reduce workplace conflict. The tension between generational cohorts, which often result from incompatible goals or misinterpretations of constructs, can lead to instability within the group dynamics (Casad & Bryant, 2016; Douglas, Howell, Nelson, Pilkington, & Salinas, 2015). If not correctly managed, generational differences can lead to misunderstanding and tensions between employees, teams, and management, thus resulting in unintended business outcomes. To create high functioning cohesive teams, leaders must be proactive in creating psychologically safe environments for bringing up healthy disputes without direct or indirect retaliation (Douglas et al., 2015). To establish common grounds for healthy communication and collaboration, a leader must also be mindful of how different generations handle and respond to conflicts.

Diffusing stereotypes. A huge part of leading a highly functioning cohesive team is managing conflict in ways that disperse stereotypes and mitigate unproductive conflict. Generational diversity can present leaders with a host of challenges due to stereotypes that often arises from varying philosophies and assumptions (Gladwell et al., 2010). These stereotypes are detrimental to working relationships and can result in a cascade of negative consequences such as impaired performance, disengagement, bias feedback, misunderstandings, resistance to feedback, reduced or problematic cooperation (Casad & Bryant, 2016; Sarooghi, Libaers, & Burkemper, 2015). However, with the appropriate interventions (training and tools) for minimizing and addressing possible strains, all employees can work side-by-side without resorting to offensive slangs, colloquialisms, or prejudicial jargons (Johnson, 2015).

Conclusion

In this chapter, the overarching keynote is that multigenerational workforce can be a competitive advantage when managed effectively through engagement and inclusion modalities as well as proactive leadership strategies. The information presented through refractive thinking can help 21st-century leaders leverage the strength of the current multigenerational workforce for organizational success and sustainable advantage. Undoubtedly, the multigenerational workforce of the 21st-century business environment has profound implications for organizations as well as leaders. The central message for organizations is clear; an inclusive and engaging culture is paramount to long-term competitive advantage and sustainable success. For leaders, the implication is to create a positively equitable, inclusive, and winning work environment for employees across all generations. To optimize the valuable intellectual capital that multigenerational employees possess, leaders need multidimensional proficiencies such as effective communication skills, team building, soft leadership skills, flexibility, tenacious performance, leadership presence, problem-solving and interpersonal alliances. To effectively lead a multigenerational labor force, leaders must exercise refractive thinking to wear multiple hats, combine interchangeable leadership paradigms, and continually evolve to meet the needs of all stakeholders.

THOUGHTS FROM THE ACADEMIC ENTREPRENEUR

The problem to be solved:

- Managing employees from several generations creates unique opportunities and challenges for organizational leaders.

The goals:

- Understanding how to accommodate intergenerational attributes and maximize the value of generational diversity through employee engagement.

The questions to ask:

- How can leaders leverage the strength of multigenerational workforce for organizational success?

- What are the best practices for cross-generational employee engagement?

Today's Business Application:

- Nuances and differences notwithstanding, every generational cohort has something to offer.

- There is no one size fit all for employees' engagement.

- Flexible and adaptive leaders will be the driving force for effectively engaging multiple generations in the workplace.

- The ability to manage conflict, diffuse stereotypes, and communicate via various channels are required to create and sustain highly functioning multigenerational teams.

REFERENCES

Al-Asfour, A., & Lettau, L. (2014). Strategies for leadership styles for multi-generational workforce. *Journal of Leadership, Accountability & Ethics, 11*(2), 58. Retrieved from http://www.na-businesspress.com/JLAE/Al-AsfourA_Web11_2_.pdf

American Institute of Architects. (2006). Generations: Dealing with boomers, gen-x, and beyond. *Practice Management Digest*. Retrieved from http://www.aia.org/nwsltr_pmcfm?pagename=pm_a_20030801_genx

André, S. (2018). Embracing generational diversity: Reducing and managing workplace conflict. *ORNAC Journal, 36*(4), 13–35. Retrieved from https://www.ornac.ca/

Anitha, J. (2014). Determinants of employee engagement and their impact on employee performance. *International Journal of Productivity and Performance, 63*, 308-323. https://dx.doi.org/10.1108/IJPPM-01-2013-0008

Arsenault, P. M. (2004). Validating generational differences: A legitimate diversity and leadership issue. *Leadership & Organization Development Journal, 25*(2), 124–141. https://dx.doi-org.ezp.waldenulibrary.org/10.1108/01437730410521813

Bagshaw, D., Lepp, M., & Zorn, C. R. (2007). International research collaboration: Building teams and managing conflicts. *Conflict Resolution Quarterly, 24*, 433–446. doi:10.1002/crq.183

Batool, B. F. (2013). Emotional intelligence and effective leadership. *Journal of Business Studies Quarterly, 4*(3), 85-94. Retrieved from http://novintarjome.com/wp-content/uploads/2013/10/March_2013_8.pdf

Benson, J., & Brown, M. (2011). Generations at work: Are there differences and do they matter? *The International Journal of Human Resource Management, 22*, 1843–1865. doi:10.1080/09585192.2011.573966

Bonfante, L. (2015). Managing multiple generations is a balancing act. *CIO Insight, 2*. Retrieved from https://www.cioinsight.com

Brandts, J., Cooper, D. J., & Weber, R. A. (2014). Legitimacy, communication, and leadership in the turnaround game. *Management Science, 61*(11), 1-44. Retrieved from: https://ddd.uab.cat/pub/worpap/2014/hdl_2072_253858/94714.pdf

Buengeler, C., Leroy, H., & De Stobbeleir, K. (2018). How leaders shape the impact of HR's diversity practices on employee inclusion. *Human Resource Management Review, 28*(3), 289–303. doi:10.1016/j.hrmr.2018.02.005

Bursch, D., & Kelly, K. (2014). Managing the multigenerational workplace. *UNC Executive Development*. Retrieved from: https://www.kenan-flagler.unc.edu/~/media/Files/documents/executive-development/managing-the-multigenerational-workplace-white-paper.pdf

Casad, B. J., Bryant, W. J. (2016). Addressing stereotype threat is critical to diversity and inclusion in organizational psychology. *Frontiers in Psychology: Organizational Psychology, 7.* doi:10.3389/fpsyg.2016.00008

Clark, K. R. (2017). Managing multiple generations in the workplace. *Radiologic Technology, 88,* 379. Retrieved From https://media.asrt.org/pdf/publications/RADT_Vol88_No4_Mammo.pdf#page=21

Dakodia, A., Rai, S., & Chawla, D. (2015). Multigenerational differences in work attributes and motivation: An empirical study. *Indian Journal of Industrial Relations, 51*(1), 81-96. Retrieved from https://www.questia.com/library/journal/1G1-463399976/multigenerational-differences-in-work-attributes

Desai, S., Rao, S., & Jabeen. S. (2018). Developing cultural intelligence: Learning together with reciprocal mentoring. *Human Resource Management International Digest, 26* (3), 38-40, https://doi.org/10.1108/HRMID-03-2018-0050

Domeyer, D. (2006). How to get the most from a multigenerational workforce. *OfficePro, 66,* 14–16. Retrieved from https://www.researchgate.net/publication/284689820_How_to_get_the_most_from_a_multigenerational_workforce

Douglas, M., Howell, T., Nelson, E., Pilkington, L., & Salinas, I. (2015). Team concepts. Improve the function of multigenerational teams. *Nursing Management, 46*(1), 11–13. doi:10.1097/01.NUMA.0000459098.71482.c4f308b781ebe7a.pdf

Fishman, A. A. (2016). How generational differences will impact America's aging workforce: strategies for dealing with aging Millennials, Generation X, and Baby Boomers. *Strategic HR Review, 15*(6), 250-257. https://dx.doi.org/10.1108/SHR-08-2016-0068

Fitch, P., & Van Brunt, B. (2016). *A guide to leadership and management in higher education: Managing across the generations.* New York, NY: Routledge.

Gichohi, P. (2014). The role of employee engagement in revitalizing creativity and innovation at the workplace: A survey of selected libraries in Meru County-Kenya. *Library Philosophy and Practice (e-journal),* 1171. Retrieved from http://digitalcommons.unl.edu/libphilprac/1171

Gladwell, N. J., Dorwart, C. E., Stone, C. F., & Hammond, C. A. (2010). Importance of and satisfaction with organizational benefits for a multigenerational workforce. *Journal of Park & Recreation Administration, 28*(2), 19. Retrieved from https://js.sagamorepub.com/jpra/article/view/1261

Goldsmith, M., Greenberg, C., Robertson, A., & Hu-Chan, M. (2003). *Global leadership: The next generation.* Upper Saddle River, NJ: Financial Times Prentice Hall.

Gutierrez, B., & Klein, D. (2017). Embracing the diverse environment in the workplace. *Issues in Information Systems, 18*(4), 65–69. Retrieved from http://www.iacis.org/iis/2017/4_iis_2017_65-69.pdf

Heinzerling. M. (2018). Effective leadership: Prior research vs. millennials. *Honors Program Thesis 319.* https://dx.doi.org/10.1016/j.hrmr.2018.02.005

Johnson, M. (2015). Engaging a multigenerational and multicultural workforce: One style does not suit all. *Plans & Trusts, 33*(5), 10–15. Retrieved from https://www.ifebp.org/inforequest/ifebp/0167275.pdf

Kruse, J. (2015). Managing multiple generations smoothly. *Corridor Business Journal, 11*(32), 17. Retrieved from https://www.corridorbusiness.com/managing-multiple-generations-smoothly/

Lee, P., Kippenbrock, T., & Emory, J. (2019). The changing face in the workplace: The arrival of the millennials. http://dx.doi.org/10.1016/j.leaqua.2012.09.001

Levenberg, P., & Aaron, M. (2018). The millennials in medicine: Tips for teaching the next generation of physicians. *Journal of Academic Ophthalmology, 10*(01), e38-e40. doi:10.1055/s-0037-1620235

Loerzel, T. (2019). Smashing the barriers to employee engagement. *Journal of Accountancy, 227*(1), 1–6. Retrieved from https://www.journalofaccountancy.com/issues/2019/jan/employee-engagement-and-retention.html

McManus Warnell, J. (2015). *Engaging millennials for ethical leadership: What works for young professionals and their managers.* New York, NY: Business Expert Press, LLC.

Mone, E. M., & London, M. (2018). Employee engagement through effective performance management. doi:10.4324/9781315626529

Naim, M. F., & Lenkla, U. (2016). Knowledge sharing as an intervention for Gen Y employees' intention to stay. *Industrial and Commercial Training, 48*(3), 142–148. doi:10.1108/ict-01-2015-0011

Neville, P. (2018). The next generation of teamwork. *People & Strategy, 41*(2), 11–13. Retrieved from https://go.galegroup.com/ps/anonymous?id=-GALE%7CA535943000&sid=googleScholar&v=2.1&it=r&linkaccess=abs&issn=19464606&p=AONE&sw=w

Nichols, T., & Wright, M. (2018). *Generational differences: Understanding and exploring generation.* 2017-2018 Officers President President-Elect, 177. NY: Hungry Minds.

Osborne, S., & Hammoud, M.S. (2017). Effective employee engagement in the workplace. *International Journal of Applied Management & Technology, 16*(1), 50–67. doi:10.5590/IJAMT.2017.16.1.04

PR Newswire. (2019, February 13). 7 employee engagement trends to expect this year. PR Newswire US. Retrieved from https://www.prnewswire.com/news-releases/7-employee-engagement-trends-to-expect-this-year-300794459.html

Sahraee, R., & Abdullah, H. B. (2017). Managing the value gap among generations in organizations: Socio-psychological approach. *International Journal of Academic Research in Business and Social Sciences, 7*(8). doi:10.6007/ijarbss/v7-i8/3276

Salahuddin, M. M. (2010). Generational differences impact on leadership style and organizational success. *Journal of Diversity Management, 5*(2), 1-6. doi:10.19030/jdm.v5i2.805

Sarooghi, H., Libaers, D., & Burkemper, A. (2015). Examining the relationship between creativity and innovation: A meta-analysis of organizational, cultural, and environmental factors. *Journal of Business Venturing, 30*, 714-731. https://dx.doi.org/10.1016/j.jbusvent.2014.12.003

Savino, E. M. (2017). Quick! How do I deal with a multigenerational workforce? *Strategic HR Review, 16*(4), 192–193. https://dx.doi-org.ezp.waldenulibrary.org/10.1108/SHR-09-2016-0087

Shatto, B., & Erwin, K. (2017). Teaching millennials and generation Z: Bridging the generational divide. *Creative Nursing, 23*(1), 24–28. doi:10.1891/1078-4535.23.1.24

Society for Human Resource Management (SHRM). (2004). Leadership styles series part ii: Leadership styles. *Society of Human Resource Management.* Retrieved from http://multigenshrmindia.org/resources/articles/leadership-styles-series-part-ii-leadership-styles- generational-differences

The Pew Research Center (2019). Defining generations: Where Millennials end and Generation Z begins. Retrieved from https://pewrsr.ch/2szqtJz

U.S. Department of Commerce. (2011). Traditionalists, Boomers, X'ers, and Nexters-NOAA's generational diversity at work. National Oceanic and Atmospheric Administration, U.S. Department of Commerce. Retrieved from http://www.rdc.naoo.gov/~Diversity/genarticle.html

Whittenburg, E., & Rogers, K. (2018). Managing multiple generations within your department or team. *Tax Executive, (2)*, 18. Retrieved from https://pdfs.semanticscholar.org/ca38/4aeba48333372ffcdbfdd4

Wiedmer, T. (2015). Generations do differ: Best practices in leading traditionalists, boomers, and generations X, Y, and Z. *Delta Kappa Gamma Society International, 82*(1). Retrieved from https://www.questia.com/library/journal/1P3-3971765321/generations-do-differ-best-practices-in-leading-traditionalists

William, K., & Page, R. A. (2011). Marketing to the generations. *Journal of Behavioral Studies in Business, 3*(1), 37-53. Retrieved from http://www.aabri.com/manuscripts/10575.pdf

Williams, A. (2015). Move over millennials, here comes generation Z. *New York Times.* http://blogs.vsb.bc.ca/sjames/files/2012/10/Move-Over-Millennials-Here-Comes-Generation-Z-The-New-York-Times.pdf

About the Authors...

Dr. Gail Ade is an ICF credentialed & Board Certified Executive Leadership, Business & Career Coach. Through intentional engagement, She facilitates breakthrough coaching to empower executive leaders (current and emerging), small business owners, professionals, and entrepreneurs to achieve sustainable success. As a social change advocate, Dr. Gail also partners with organizations to advance diversity beyond representation.

Dr. Gail earned her Doctor of Business Administration (DBA) in Organizational Leadership, and Master of Business Administration (MBA) in Human Resource Management. She also holds a Ph.D. Bridge to Management in Leadership & Organizational Strategy, as well as a Graduate Certificate in Industrial & Organizational Psychology.

Dr. Gail is an active member of the Society for Human Resource Management (SHRM), International Coach Federation (ICF), National Society of Leadership & Success, and Society for Diversity.

To reach Dr. Gail Ade, please **e-mail:** dradegail@gmail.com

Dr. Tokunbo A. Majaro resides in the historic town of Ewing, NJ. Dr. Majaro holds several accredited degrees: a Master of Science (MS) in Healthcare Administration; and a Doctorate (Ph.D.) in Health Services-Public Health Policy from Walden University. His experience spans working on and managing clinical trials for biopharmaceutical companies with domestic and global operations. He is passionate about the success of organizational leaders. Dr. Tokunbo also provides professional coaching services to health care executives on effective leadership strategies.

Dr. Tokunbo is an active member of the American College of Healthcare Executives and the National Society of Leadership & Success.

To reach Dr. Tokunbo Majaro, please **e-mail:** drtmajaro@gmail.com

Dr. Marietta Poshi resides in Clearwater, FL with her family. She is the Business Program Director for Keiser University, the Clearwater Campus. She is a professor with Keiser University, Everglades University, and Saint Petersburg College. She serves in the Teaching and Learning Committee, Marketing Committee, as well as the Assessment Committee for Keiser University. She belongs to the international scientific board for the International Institute for Private, Commercial, and Competition Law, their editorial board for the peer-review journal, and Conference.

Dr. Marietta Poshi holds a Doctor of Business Administration (DBA) in Marketing from Northcentral University, Master of Accountancy (MAcc) from Keiser University, and Master of Business Administration (MBA) in Business & Marketing from Keller Graduate School of Management.

To reach Dr. Marietta Poshi, please **e-mail:** drmposhi@gmail.com

CHAPTER 9

Fundamentals of Success Through Generations

Dr. Teresa Sanders & Dr. Cheryl Lentz

The purpose of compulsory education, as envisioned by public education advocate Horace Mann (1796-1859), was to establish a social learning system to teach American youth the moral and cultural standards of society (as cited in Spring, 2011; Warder, 2015). Evolving over time, schools became community hubs to address social concerns such as racial inequality, poverty, and workforce preparation (Ravitch, 2013; Warder, 2015). The challenge in 2019 is the inability for schools to maintain and achieve their mission. The goal for this writing is to use a refractive thinking lens to explore how society might use a back-to-basics strategy to return to its original mission to educate and prepare learners to be productive citizens (Brookfield, 1987, 1991).

According to Alexander and Alexander (2005), Mann (1837) believed political and social stability depended on (a) education as the core of noble citizenship, (b) participation in democracy, and (c) the good of society overall. Mann (1843) stated, "Common School may be the most useful and benevolent of all forces of civilization" (as cited in Alexander & Alexander, 2005, p. 29; Warder, 2015). The vision of public school, as perceived by Mann (1837), evolved into an entity that scarcely resembles education in his day begging the question, what went so wrong?

Contemporary schooling has taken on a different ideal that reflects a business model rather than the societal focus envisioned by Mann (1837) (as cited in Ravitch, 2013; Warder, 2015).

Considering the vast shift in direction from teaching the nation's youth societal expectations to pursuing ranking and status determined by test scores, stakeholders must consider the social and academic outcomes sacrificed with this evolution of public education into the business model. How does one address the *business* of education and the student with such a consumer focus? The paradigm shift to the *consumer learner* (Silver & Lentz, 2005), needs to address the shortcomings of such an educational system based on a transactional exchange (instead of a transformative one) and the unintended consequences negatively impacting the original foundational and fundamental goals.

The goal of this chapter is to explore how the evolution of the business of academia model misses the mark of the intention of educating children to become productive future adults (and citizens in Brookfield's language). One need only look at the recent college admissions scandal as confirmation that all is not well even in institutions of higher learning (Friedman, 2019). A need exists for alternative solutions based in refractive thinking to change direction with a return to educational fundamentals as suggested by Mann (1837) and Brookfield (1987, 1991).

Fundamentals of Success Over Generations

According to Ruth Henderson (2018), it's an old cliché, "What gets measured gets done." The origin of the statement is up for debate; it seems that the original phrase was actually "If you can measure it, you can manage it" (Henderson, 2018, para. 1). The question asked, is whether this axiom of measurement focus is true. Is clarity of purpose enough? Is academia measuring the right key performance indicators? Our contention is no.

The road forward with a *back-to-the-basics* focus is wrought with agency imposed obstacles to genuine student achievement. Measurement does not get the job done. The public school system appears to be stuck in a cycle of failure, disguised as accountability. Education policy makers and professionals fell into the lock-step ranks of *preparing* students for standardized testing as a key performance indicator, while neglecting the overarching needs of students who lack the skills to pass grade-level tests. The focus is wrong. The outcome is wrong.

Despite the reality that students may be two, three, or more grade levels behind where they should be, the school year is spent preparing students to take tests that data, teacher input and common sense indicates they will not pass. Millennials and Generation Xers are those affected most by the questionably effective use of standardized testing (Popham, 1999). Society has generations of data that proves the question is legitimate.

Educators spend time with students day in and day out during the school year. Educational professionals know when students lack the skills needed to pass a test. Yet, as professionals, their judgment is discounted or ignored completely, mandated by the state (any of the 50 in the United States) to prepare students to test on grade level. Teachers are literally mandated by the system to set students up to fail.

Rather than subjecting *under-* or *un*prepared students for a test they cannot pass, perhaps educators and policymakers could consider alternatives that meet under-resourced students' needs by *gauging growth* as opposed to passing a test. Business stakeholders would never continue to tolerate such dismal results and remain in business. Why do we accept such results here? In business, unprofitable line items are corrected, adjusted, or removed. Shareholders will not tolerate unprofitability. The business of academia is not profitable. Why not treat the business of teaching children in the same manner?

Refractive Thinking Suggestions

Ideally, all students regardless of age or grade level, should participate in a comprehensive curriculum; however, all students may not be prepared to participate *successfully*. The following research data indicated the statistical likelihood of academic failure in the futures of under-prepared students. A review of the unacceptable and alarming National Center for Education Statistics (NCES) (2017) statistics indicated an alarming 75% or three million out of four million fourth graders, in America read below grade level. As a result, 7 out of 10 of these students will continue to struggle with any reading content presented to them on grade level (National Center for Education Statistics [NCES], 2017). Two thirds of that 70% will drop out of high school before completion or will not be prepared to be productive in the workplace (NCES, 2017). Welfare, incarceration, and poverty await most students who drop out of school (U.S. Department of Justice, 2015). A skilled American workforce may not be available to the business world particularly in the sciences, widening the gap in future generations' ability to meet the business needs of society.

Knowing what awaits students who do not achieve academically should encourage educators and policymakers to review public school policy. Hopefully, they will commit to making the necessary adjustments to meet the needs of all learners. Students who are behind academically would benefit from mastering the basics of academic success as proffered by Mann (1837) and Brookfield (1987, 1991); reading, writing, and math skills, *before* exploring other curriculum content.

The rationale for this suggestion is simple. Students at risk of social and academic failure must minimally learn to read, write, and do basic math computations. Without these skills, securing gainful employment will be nearly impossible. Without gainful employment, dependence on entitlements, substance use, criminal activity, or incarceration will be among the likely outcomes for these students (U.S. Department of Justice, 2018). Institutions of higher learning have begun looking at competency-based learning or skills based learning in an effort to teach students based on what they know (Fain, 2014). Perhaps this change in curriculum should be considered at the lower grade levels in elementary education for future generations as well.

Social studies, science, or music would be positive contributions to low performing students' academic repertoires. However, from a harm reduction perspective, it is infinitely more important that these students learn to read, write, and perform basic math calculations to help them to function effectively as adults (Mann, 1837; Brookfield, 1987, 1991; Silver & Lentz, 2005). To spend valuable instruction time on content that will not help academically struggling students succeed remains counterproductive to our goals as educators, not to mention exactly the opposite of what businesses would do to stay in business. One does not continue to invest in a losing commodity. Social studies is not a priority when students cannot read. Prioritizing foundational skills over comprehensive content is a must. These students may not be able to identify Kansas on a map, but they will be able to tell time, count change, fill out a job application, and build practical skills for the workplace.

Policymakers

With more than 50 years of noted failure of educational reform efforts and negligible improvement in student achievement (NCES, 2011), now is the time to review and revise public education policies. Revision must happen in a way that meets the diverse needs of contemporary learners, particularly those behind academically. Struggling students must learn the academic basics they will need to function effectively as adults (Elias, 2009).

The literacy crisis in America's public schools demonstrates the need to revisit the efficacy of state testing students on grade level, though students could be multiple grade levels behind. If education is a business, then let us treat it as such. Expectations must be results driven. Activity is not productivity. Efforts are not outcomes. The focus must only be on results that drive progress as well as process. The academic priority for fourth grade students functioning below grade level must be acquisition of the basic skills necessary to participate successfully in school and the workforce. Policies that allow assessment of students on their present performance levels will likely result in measurable improvement in academic and social achievement (National Research Council, 2011).

This harm reduction approach to low-performing students (ensuring they learn minimally to read, write and complete math operations) may provide students an opportunity to develop the basic skills needed to function positively as adults (Wexler, 2018), such as counting money, calculating time, making change, or reading instructions. Without the ability to read, write, or complete basic math calculations, subjects such as social studies, science, art, and music should be considered content that will be postponed until basic skills are mastered, supporting a competency skills based learning model as applied at the college level. This recommendation is not meant to suggest the latter-mentioned subjects lack usefulness or value in an ideal learning circumstance. In contrast, we are saying the exact opposite. When a student reaches the point he or she is unlikely to ever catch up academically, the need to read, write, and calculate basic math operations must take priority over more comprehensive content. Brookfield (1987, 1991) reminds us of the focus on these fundamentals leading to the goal of producing productive and contributing members of society.

What is our goal of educating our students? Why cannot the vision match specific implementation of the mission statement and follow the business model? The consumer learner needs to fight back to demand higher quality and return on investment (ROI) (Silver & Lentz, 2005).

Participation in grade level standardized testing for students performing below grade level, should be eliminated. Testing these students will not produce useful results and serves only to demoralize testers when they fail (Moon, Brighton, Jarvis, & Hall, 2007). Let accountability be measured in student-specific growth rather than one-size-fits-all standardized tests. Student-centered policies could possibly allow educators the flexibility they need to help low performing students succeed by meeting them where they are academically, rather than preparing them to take an assessment they cannot pass.

Administrators

Effective student achievement can become a reality instead of back-to-school convocation rhetoric. If what gets measured gets done, let us focus on measuring effective learning skills, not test-taking data. Ensuring the early identification of struggling students (le Cordur, 2010), providing effective remediation (McCusker, 1999), not promoting before mastering grade level content (McCallister, 2014) and focusing curriculum content on literacy building material (Concordia University-Portland, 2018), may help struggling students catch up. If students cannot or do not catch up to grade level, perhaps at the very least, students can exit school able to read, write, and complete basic math calculations, building a pathway to effective citizenry.

Campus administrators can take steps to switch from the *pass the test* mindset to a *harm reduction* perspective to ensure the most at-risk students can leave school with at least the foundational skills needed to maintain a living for themselves. Educational decisions must serve the best interest of the students for their end goal of effective citizenry. At the campus level, perhaps the focus of the most at-risk learners could be on basic skills when it has been determined they are not likely to pass the state assessment because of their current academic deficiencies.

Educators

Preparing for standardized testing leaves little instruction time for teachers to focus on anything not covered on the test. Despite this limitation, all educators can contribute to the academic growth of students, especially those who are under-resourced. Research indicated when students share positive relationships with teachers and school staff, academic outcomes are improved and discipline and dropouts are reduced (University of Cambridge, 2016).

Active parental involvement in their children's education affects positively student behavior, social interactions, reduces truancy, and improves school satisfaction (Fraser-Thill, 2018). One of the first and most effective contributions teachers can make to all students' achievement is to ensure parents know their involvement with their children's teachers is invaluable (National Parent Teacher Association, 2018). Developing positive mutually beneficial relationships with parents is a must to realize optimal social and academic outcomes with students (McQuiggan, Megra, & Grady, 2017; National Parent Teacher Association, 2018).

Educators can model for and continually expect social and academic excellence from all students (Hanover Research, 2012). Teachers cannot control the folly that may be inherent in students' homes and lives or standardized testing, but they can contribute to any child's success through positive interactions (National Parent Teacher Association, 2018) and using data to direct instruction (Fenton & Murphy, 2019).

Parents

The role of parents in education is the most important of all stakeholders (Urban Child Institute, 2013). Parents can partner with their children's teachers by communicating the importance of education and by reinforcing what is expected of them as it relates to learning in and outside of the classroom. When teachers and parents communicate regularly student achievement improves, negative behavior decreases, students report higher feelings of self-esteem and more motivation to learn (Perkins, 2015).

Reading to children exposes them to vocabulary, stimulates their imaginations, introduces them to spelling, conventions of writing, and other benefits (Bonfiglio, 2017). All parents can maximize their children's achievement simply by reading to them. A minimum of 20 minutes per day is the suggested amount of time to net potential academic benefits from reading at home, however; any time spent reading is better than none (K12Reader, 2018).

In low-income households, this is particularly critical. According to the NCES (2011), children who live in poverty are less likely to be read to at home. For low-income parents and children, making daily reading a priority in their homes increases the likelihood their children will become proficient readers (NCES, 2011).

In addition to maintaining a literacy rich environment in the home, parents are encouraged to collaborate with their children's teachers regularly. According to the National Parent Teacher Association (PTA) (2018), a significant indicator of student achievement is the degree families are involved in their children's education. Parental involvement is a cost effective and immediate way to potentially improve student achievement.

Parents could benefit from becoming familiar with the state mandated skills their children are required to learn. Rather than celebrating good grades on report cards, parents should assess whether their children have mastered the skills their grades reflect. In the increasingly common event that student achievement stands in contrast to student grade reports, parents can share their findings with their children's' teachers and work collaboratively to ensure students continue to learn with accurate achievement reflected in their grades.

All parents and interested stakeholders are encouraged to visit their children's or neighborhood schools throughout the school year from time-to-time. An hour or so of walking the campuses and meeting the faculty may allow stakeholders an opportunity to gauge the campus atmosphere, observe educators in action, participate in campus activities, and ask any questions they may have. Progressive administrators should welcome parent and community input and value their presence on campuses.

Shutting Down the School-to-Prison Pipeline

Negative behavior is very common when students are academically incompetent (Miller, 2009). Classroom disruptions and insubordination often result when frustrated students cannot keep up in class. These behaviors often result in multiple suspensions from school, which can inadvertently place students on a path to incarceration, often described as the *school-to-prison pipeline.* The school-to-prison pipeline refers to the process of disciplining students by removing them from school and connecting them to law enforcement (Nelson & Lind, 2015) or correctional-related facilities (Cheek & Bucchio, 2017). In doing so, students are subsequently criminalized by disciplinary practices in schools. Zero tolerance rules employed by many districts are often cited as a major contributor to the school-to-prison pipeline (Cheek & Bucchio, 2017).

According to Cheek and Bucchio (2017), the elimination of the school-to-prison pipeline is an immediate nationwide priority. By reducing academic incompetence, it is possible to reduce and in some cases, eliminate the maladaptive behavior that results from academic failure. By ending the practice of presenting students with work and tests they lack the skills to complete, schools could take a monumental step towards shutting down the school-to-prison pipeline and opening a pathway to potential achievement.

Conclusion

Five decades of education reform and its impact on generations and the connection between fourth grade reading skills and high school completion was explored in this chapter. The 2017 fourth grade reading performance of America's students as captured in the International Reading and Literacy Study (PIRLS) indicated that out of four million American fourth graders, three million cannot read proficiently.

There exists a strong correlation between low reading in the fourth grade and dropping out of high school. The consequences of academic failure and dropping out of school was examined and the potential social and professional consequences that follow for adults who cannot read well was addressed. Stakeholders were offered suggestions for possible remediation which included policy changes at the state level, flexibility and reallocation of time and resources at the campus level, and robust involvement in learning in the home. The urgent need to reduce the flow to the school-to-prison pipeline remains a priority. Perhaps a commitment from state policymakers to reconsider academic priorities can be the first step towards reducing the flow of the school-to-prison pipeline to a trickle.

The challenge is the inability of schools to maintain and achieve their mission of educating America's students. The goal of this writing was to look at the refractive thinking perspective of asking the question of how society can help get education back on track and back-to-basics to educate the current and future generations to prepare them to be productive members of society.

THOUGHTS FROM THE ACADEMIC ENTREPRENEUR

The problem to be solved:

- Declining literacy skills among students in America's public schools and mitigation of the social and professional consequences that follow.

The goals:

- To explore academic alternatives for students not reading on grade level.

The questions to ask:

- Why are we accepting academic failure given all the resources afforded to students in the United States and the social and fiscal costs associated with academic failure?

- Can a harm reduction approach mitigate some of the negative outcomes associated with academic failure?

Today's Business Application:

- Basic literacy skills are required to function successfully in school and the workplace. When students fail to master reading, writing and basic math skills, taxpayers bear the costs associated with academic failure. Those costs flow from increased dependence on welfare entitlements, criminal justice contacts, unemployment, substance abuse etc. Businesses and even the military suffer when new recruits lack the basic skills needed to function effectively in their respective roles forcing them to offer remedial training that new recruits should master in elementary school.

- Persistent failure in our nation's schools puts the United States at a disadvantage when attempting to compete in an increasingly global business environment. A lack of qualified American students can result in outsourcing of domestic jobs and increased professional and academic talent recruiting from outside of the United States.

REFERENCES

Alexander, K., & Alexander, M. (2005). *American public school law*. Retrieved from https://books.google.com/books?id=BkZfdC-wvMC&pg=PA29&lpg=PA29&dq=%E2%80%9CCommon+School

A nation at risk: The imperative for educational reform. (1983, April). A report to the nation and the Secretary of Education U.S. Department of Education by The National Commission on Excellence in Education, April 1983. Retrieved from https://www2.ed.gov/pubs/NatAtRisk/risk.html

Association for the Education of Young Children. (n.d.). *Developmentally appropriate practices for young children*. Retrieved from http://www.readingrockets.org/article/goals-first-grade-early-reading-and-writing

Bonfiglio, C. (2017). 10 Benefits that highlight the importance of reading with young children. Retrieved from https://bilingualkidspot.com/2017/10/19/benefits-importance-reading-young-children/

Brookfield, S. D. (1987). *Developing critical thinkers: Challenging adults to explore alternative ways of thinking and acting*. San Francisco, CA: Jossey-Bass Publishers.

Brookfield, D. (1991). *Understanding and facilitating adult learning*. San Francisco, CA: Jossey-Bass.

Cleveland, H. (2015). *Why reading by fourth grade matters for student success*. Retrieved from https://readingpartners.org/blog/why-reading-by-fourth-grade-matters-for-student-success/

Cheek, K., & Bucchio, J. (2017). *School-to-prison pipeline can be dismantled using alternative discipline strategies*. Retrieved from https://youthtoday.org/2017/09/school-to-prison-pipeline-can-be-dismantled-using-alternative-discipline-strategies/

Concordia University-Portland. (2018). *The state of literacy in America*. Retrieved from https://education.cu-portland.edu/blog/education-news-roundup/illiteracy-in-america/

Education Consumers Foundation. (2016). *Fiscal effect of reading failure*. Retrieved from http://education-consumers.org/research-areas/consumer-tools/ecf-cost-calculator-information/

Elias, M. (2009). The four keys to helping at-risk kids. *Edutopia*. Retrieved from https://www.edutopia.org/strategies-help-at-risk-students

Fandel, L. (2012). *If a child can't read in fourth grade*. Retrieved from https://iowaeducation.iowa.gov/2012/01/12/if-a-child-can%E2%80%99t-read-in-fourth-grade

Fenton, B., & Murphy, M. (2019). *Data-driven instruction*. Retrieved from http://www.ascd.org/ascd-express/vol5/508-fenton.aspx

Findlaw Online. (2014). *Compulsory education laws: Background*. Retrieved from https://education.findlaw.com/education-options/compulsory-educa-tion-laws-background.html

Fraser-Thill, R. (2018). *How parental involvement benefits kids*. Retrieved from https://www.verywellfamily.com/how-parent-involvement-benefits-kids-3288064

Friedman, Z. (2019). *30 fast facts about the college admission scandal*. Retrieved from https://www.forbes.com/sites/zackfriedman/2019/03/18/30-facts-college-admissions-scandal/#638de35312a0

Hanover Research. (2012). *High expectations and student success*. Retrieved from https://danhaesler.com/wp-content/uploads/2015/02/High-Expectations-Mindset.pdf

Henderson, R. (2015, June 8). What gets measured gets done. Or does it? *Forbes Online*. Retrieved from https://www.forbes.com/sites/ellevate/2015/06/08/what-gets-measured-gets-done-or-does-it/#73bb8ae613c8

Jacobsen, R., & Rothstein, R. (2006). The goals of education. *Economic Policy Institute. Phi Delta Kappan, 88*(4), 264-272. Retrieved from https://www.epi.org/publication/webfeatures_viewpoints_education_goals/

K12 Reader. (2018). *Why read 20 minutes?* Retrieved from http://www.k12reader.com

Katsiyannis, A., Ryan, J., Zhang, D., & Spann, A. (2008). Juvenile delinquency and recidivism: The impact of academic achievement. *Taylor and Francis online*. https://dx.doi.org/10.1080/10573560701808460

Kirk, D. S., & Sampson, R. J. (2012). Juvenile arrest and collateral educational damage in the transition to adulthood. *Sociology of Education, 88*(1), 36-62. doi:10.1177/0038040712448862

Le Cordeur, M. (2010). The struggling reader: Identifying and addressing reading problems successfully at an early age. *Per Linguam Journal, 26*(2), 77-89. http://dx.doi.org/10.5785/26-2-23

McQuiggan, M., Megra, M., & Grady, S. (2017). *Parent and family involvement in education: Results from the national household surveys program of 2016*. Retrieved from https://nces.ed.gov/pubs2017/2017102.pdf

Moran, R. N. (2009). Education reform: An analysis of the purpose and function of public education. *University of Tennessee Honors Thesis Projects*. Retrieved from https://trace.tennessee.edu/utk_chanhonoproj/1300

Miller, R. (2009). Student performance: Conduct and behavior concerns. *International Journal of Teaching and Learning in Higher Education, 21(2)*, 248-251.

McCusker, M. (1999). ERIC Review: Effective elements of developmental reading and writing Programs. *Community College Review, 27*(2), 93–105. https://dx.doi.org/10.1177/009155219902700205

Moon, T. R., Brighton, C. M., Jarvis, J. M., & Hall, C. J. (2007). Standardized testing programs: Their effects on students and teachers. *National Research Center for the Gifted and Talented.* Retrieved from https://nrcgt.uconn.edu/wp-content/uploads/sites/953/2015/04/rm07228.pdf

National Center for Education Statistics (NCES). (2011). *Three decades of student performance.* Retrieved from https://nces.ed.gov/nationsreportcard/pubs/main1999/2000469.asp

National Center for Education Statistics (NCES). (2017). *Reading achievement of U.S. fourth-grade students in an international context.* Retrieved from https://nces.ed.gov/pubsearch/pubsinfo.asp?pubid=2018017

National Parent Teacher Association. (2018). *Parent's guide to student success.* Retrieved from https://www.pta.org/

Neill, M., & Guisbond, G. (2004). *Failing our children.* Retrieved from http://www.fairtest.org/failing_Our_Children_Report.html

Nelson, L., & Lind, D. (2015). *The school to prison pipeline explained.* Retrieved from http://www.justicepolicy.org/news/8775

National Research Council. (2001*). Knowing what students know: The science and design of educational assessment.* Washington, DC: The National Academies Press. https://dx.doi.org/10.17226/10019.

Perkins, K. (2015). Parents and teachers working together. *Acer Research Developments.* Retrieved from https://rd.acer.org/article/parents-and-teachers-working-together

Popham, W. J. (1999, March). Why standardized tests don't measure education quality. *Educational Leadership, 56*(6), 8-15.

Popham, W. J. (2001). *Teaching to the test?* Retrieved from http://www.ascd.org/publications/educational-leadership/mar01/vol58/num06/Teaching-to-the-Test%C2%A2.aspx

ProCon. (2018). *Is the use of standardized tests improving education in America?* Retrieved from https://standardizedtests.procon.org/

Silver, G., & Lentz, C. (2005). *The consumer learner: Emerging expectations of a customer service mentality in post-secondary education.* Las Vegas, NV: Pensiero Press.

Smithsonian National Museum of American History. (2017). *Separate is not equal: Brown v. Board of Education is a collective effort of the staff of the National Museum of American History, Behring Center.* Retrieved from http://americanhistory.si.edu/brown/history/1-segregated/separate-but-equal.html

Sparks, D. (2012*). Students who struggle early rarely catch up study says.* Retrieved from http://blogs.edweek.org/edweek/inside-schoolresearch/2012/12/Helping_struggling_students_catch_up.html

Ratvich, D. (1990). Education in the 1980s: A concern for quality. *Education Week.* Retrieved from https://www.edweek.org/ew/articles/1990/01/10/09200009.h09.html

Urban Child Institute. (2013). *Parents: The most important teachers.* Retrieved from http://www.urbanchildinstitute.org/articles/perceptions/parents-the-most-important-teachers

U.S. Department of Justice. (2015). *Title IX of the Education Amendments of 1972.* Retrieved from https://www.justice.gov/crt/title-ix-education-amendments-1972

U.S. Department of Labor. (2012). *Section 504, Rehabilitation Act of 1973.* Retrieved from https://www.dol.gov/oasam/regs/statutes/sec504.htm

University of Cambridge. (2016). *Positive teacher-student relationships boost good behavior in teenagers for up to four years.* Retrieved from https://www.cam.ac.uk/research/news/positive-teacher-student-relationships-boost-good-behaviour-in-teenagers-for-up-to-four-years

Warder, G. (2015). *Horace Mann and the creation of the Common School.* Retrieved from http://www.disabilitymuseum.org/dhm/edu/essay.html?id=42.

Wexler, N. (2018). Why American students haven't gotten better at reading in 20 years. *The Atlantic.* Retrieved from https://www.theatlantic.com/education/archive/2018/04/-american-students-reading/557915/

About the Authors . . .

Dr. Teresa Sanders earned a doctoral degree in Educational Leadership from the University of Phoenix in 2007. She has 20 years of experience in mental health / science services and has been an educator for 13 years. Currently, Dr. Teresa teaches in a rural, but expanding district in North Texas. Additionally, Dr. Teresa spent 12 years as an adjunct faculty member for the University of Phoenix.

Dr. Teresa works successfully with the most marginalized and challenging populations by taking a holistic, comprehensive approach to interacting with students and families and welcoming parents as allies in their children's education. She is an advocate for students and parents in the school environment and believes for students to demonstrate maximum academic achievement, parents must be engaged actively in effective school-home partnerships.

Dr. Teresa has presented at international education conferences, writes weekly education articles for three newspapers and endeavors to develop a comprehensive education program to meet the needs of the most academically at-risk students.

To reach Dr. Teresa Sanders for additional information **e-mail:** teresa esanders@gmail.com

Dr. Cheryl A. Lentz affectionately known as Doc C to her students, is a university professor on faculty with Embry-Riddle University, Grand Canyon University (GCU), University of Phoenix, and Walden University. Dr. Cheryl serves as a dissertation mentor / chair and committee member. She is also a dissertation coach, offering expertise as a professional editor for APA style for graduate thesis and doctoral dissertations, as well as journal publications and books.

Dr. Cheryl holds a BA in Music History from the University of Illinois, Champaign-Urbana, a MSIR with a specialization in International Relations from Troy University, and a Doctorate of Management in Organizational Leadership. Dr. Cheryl is a public speaker at many universities across the United States and in

Europe, as well as consults with corporations on leadership, marketing, and publishing.

Awards include: Walden Faculty of the Year, DBA Program, 2016, UOP community service award, and 18 writing awards.

Dr. Cheryl is also an active member of Alpha Sigma Alpha Sorority.

She is an international best-selling author with more than 39 publications known for her writings on *The Golden Palace Theory of Management* and refractive thinking. Additional published works include her dissertation: *Strategic Decision Making in Organizational Performance, Journey Outside the Golden Palace, The Consumer Learner, Technology That Tutors, Effective Study Skills, The Dissertation Toolbox,* International Best Seller *The Expert Success Solution,* and contributions to the award-winning series *The Refractive Thinker®: Anthology of Doctoral Learners, Volumes I–XVI.*

To reach Dr. Cheryl Lentz for information on refractive thinking, professional editing, radio show guest, or public speaking, please visit her **websites:** http://www.DrCherylLentz.com, http://www.LentzLeadership.com, or **e-mail:** drcheryllentz@gmail.com

Index

The
Refractive
Thinker®

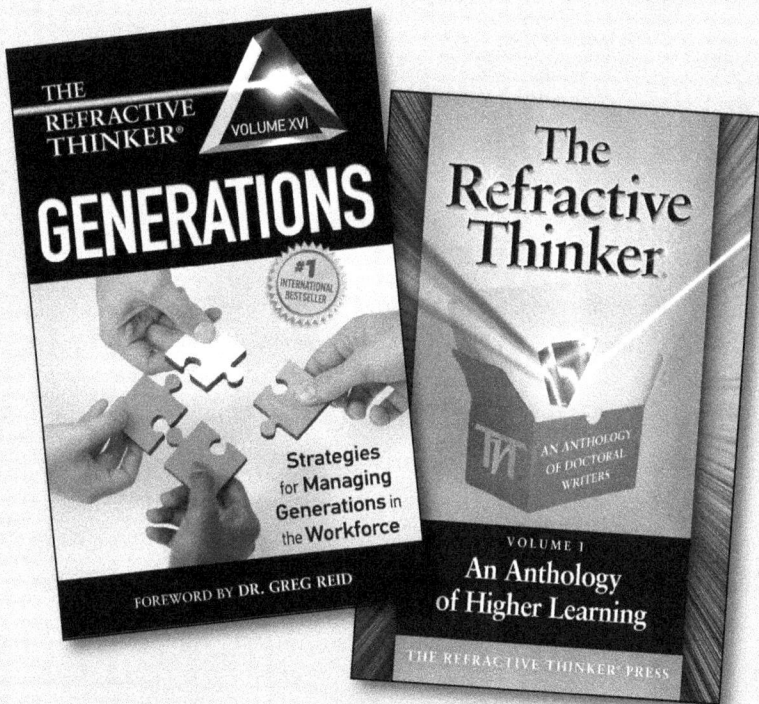

THE
REFRACTIVE
THINKER® VOLUME XVI

GENERATIONS

#1 INTERNATIONAL BESTSELLER

Strategies
for Managing
Generations in
the Workforce

FOREWORD BY DR. GREG REID

The
Refractive
Thinker®

AN ANTHOLOGY
OF DOCTORAL
WRITERS

VOLUME I
An Anthology
of Higher Learning

THE REFRACTIVE THINKER® PRESS

2019 CATALOG

The Refractive Thinker®:
An Anthology of Higher Learning

The Refractive Thinker® Press

info@refractivethinker.com
www.RefractiveThinker.com
blog: www.DissertationPublishing.com

Books are available through The Refractive Thinker® Press at special discounts for bulk purchases for the purpose of sales promotion, seminar attendance, or educational purposes. Special volumes can be created for specific purposes and to organizational specifications. Orders placed on www.RefractiveThinker.com for students and military receive a 15% discount. Please contact us for further details.

Refractive Thinker® logo by Joey Root; The Refractive Thinker® Press logo design by Jacqueline Teng, cover design by Peri Poloni-Gabriel, Knockout Design (knockoutbooks.com), cover design & production by Gary A. Rosenberg (thebookcouple.com).

> I *think* therefore I am.
> —Renee Descartes

> I *critically think* to be.
> I *refractively think* to change the world.

THANK YOU FOR JOINING US as we continue to celebrate the accomplishments of doctoral scholars affiliated with many phenomenal institutions of higher learning. The purpose of the anthology series is to share a glimpse into the scholarly works of participating authors on various subjects.

The Refractive Thinker® serves the tenets of leadership, which is not simply a concept outside of the self, but comes from within, defining our very essence; where the search to define leadership becomes our personal journey, not yet a finite destination.

The Refractive Thinker® is an intimate expression of who we are: the ability to think beyond the traditional boundaries of thinking and critical thinking. Instead of mere reflection and evaluation, one challenges the very boundaries of the constructs itself. If thinking is *inside* the box, and critical thinking is *outside* the box, we add the next step of refractive thinking, *beyond* the box. Perhaps the need exists to dissolve the box completely. The authors within these pages are on a mission to change the world. They are never satisfied or quite content with *what is* or asking *why,* instead these authors intentionally strive to push and test the limits to ask *why not.*

We look forward to your interest in discussing future opportunities. Let our collection of authors continue the journey initiated with Volume I, to which *The Refractive Thinker*® will serve as our guide to future volumes. Come join us in our quest to be refractive thinkers and add your wisdom to the collective. We look forward to your stories.

Please contact The Refractive Thinker® Press for information regarding these authors and the works contained within these pages. Perhaps you or your organization may be looking for an author's expertise to incorporate as part of your annual corporate meetings as a keynote or guest speaker(s), perhaps to offer individual, or group seminars or coaching, or require their expertise as consultants.

Join us on our continuing adventures of *The Refractive Thinker*® where we expand the discussion specifically begun in Volume I: Leadership; Volume II (Editions 1–3): Research Methodology; Volume III: Change Management; Volume IV: Ethics, Leadership, and Globalization; Volume V: Strategy in Innovation; Volume VI: Post-Secondary Education; Volume VII: Social Responsibility; Volume VIII: Effective Business Practices in Motivation & Communication; Volume IX: Effective Business Practices in Leadership & Emerging Technologies; Volume X: Effective Business Strategies for the Defense Industry Sector; Volume XI: Women in Leadership; Volume XII: Cybersecurity in an Increasingly Insecure World; Volume XIV: Healthcare: The Impact on Leadership, Business, and Education; and Volume XV: Nonprofits: Strategies for Effective Management. All our volumes are themed to explore the realm of strategic thought, creativity, and innovation.

Dr. Cheryl A. Lentz, managing editor of The Lentz Leadership Institute, explains the unique benefits of the books for readers:

"They celebrate the diffusion of innovative refractive thinking through the writings of these doctoral scholars as they dare to think differently in search of new applications and understandings of research. Unlike most academic books that merely define research, The Refractive Thinker® *offers unique appli-*  *cations of research from the perspective of multiple authors—each offering a chapter based on their specific expertise."*

THE REFRACTIVE THINKER® PRESS

Volume I: An Anthology of Higher Learning

Volume II, 1st through 3rd Editions: Research Methodology

Volume III: Change Management

Volume IV: Ethics, Leadership, and Globalization

Volume V: Strategy in Innovation

Volume VI: Post-Secondary Education

Volume VII: Social Responsibility

Volume VIII: Effective Business Practices for Motivation and Communication

Volume IX: Effective Business Practices in Leadership & Emerging Technologies

Volume X: Effective Business Strategies for the Defense Industry Sector

Volume XI: Women in Leadership

Volume XII: Cybersecurity in an Increasingly Insecure World

Volume XIII: Entrepreneurship: Growing the Future of Business

Volume XIV: Healthcare: The Impact on Leadership, Business, and Education

Volume XV: Nonprofits: Strategies for Effective Management

Volume XVI: Generations: Strategies for Managing Generations in the Workforce

Refractive Thinker volumes are available in e-book, Kindle®, iPad®, Nook®, and Sony Reader™, as well as individual e-chapters by author.

Coming Soon From the Refractive Thinker®!
AVAILABLE THRU THE LENTZ LEADERSHIP INSTITUTE
The Refractive Thinker®: Vol XVII: Managing a Cultural Workforce

Telephone orders: Call us at 702.719.9214

Email Orders: drcheryllentz@gmail.com

Website orders: Please place orders through our website:
www.RefractiveThinker.com

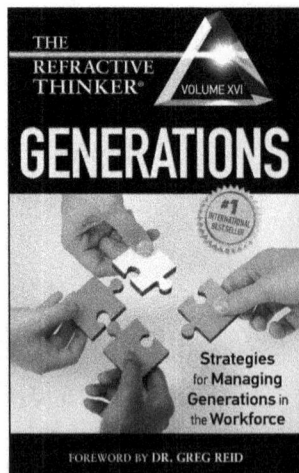

#1 INTERNATIONAL BEST SELLER!

The Refractive Thinker® Volume XV: Nonprofits: Strategies for Effective Management

In this key volume, contributing scholars discuss research focused on nonprofit organizations and their specific needs regarding strategies for effective management. This volume continues to shape the conversation of their future success and the latest best practices and proven strategies for success.

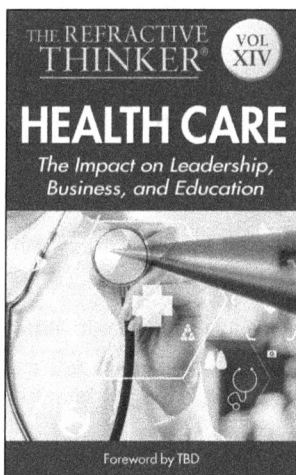

THE REFRACTIVE THINKER®
VOLUME XV

NONPROFITS

STRATEGIES FOR EFFECTIVE MANAGEMENT

#1 International Best Seller

10th Anniversary Edition

FOREWORD BY
FRANK SHANKWITZ
Founder of The Make-a-Wish Foundation

THE REFRACTIVE THINKER® VOL XIV

HEALTH CARE
The Impact on Leadership, Business, and Education

Foreword by TBD

#1 AMAZON BEST SELLER!

The Refractive Thinker®: Volume XIV: Health Care: The Impact on Leadership, Business, and Education

Dr. Gladys Taylor McGarey is internationally known for her pioneer work in alternative medicine. She says it is not about killing off a disease, but seeing the patient as a whole person. She believes that the practice of medicine has become a war against disease—rather than building life, we are destroying it. As we support the living process in a person, life itself brings about the healing that the person needs. Our job as physicians is to work and support the "Physician Within" each of us. Then, living medicine becomes our dwelling place.

For more information, please visit our website: www.RefractiveThinker.com

The Refractive Thinker®: Volume XIII:
Entrepreneurship: Growing the Future
of Business

Join Clarissa Burt and contributing scholars as they discuss current research regarding the future of business and the influence of the entrepreneur. This volume contains research shaping the conversation on what the future may hold to success of the economy in the hands of the emerging and evolving small business owner and entrepreneur. As you read, ask yourself: "What should I be doing as an entrepreneur to contribute to the world economy as well as my own success?" Be a refractive thinker as part of the solution to reap the benefits promised in this new digital age.

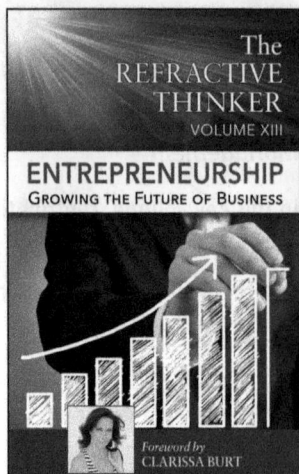

The Refractive Thinker®: Volume XII:
Cybersecurity in an Increasingly
Insecure World

Join contributing scholars as they discuss current research regarding the challenges of the world of cybersecurity and its effects in and on the marketplace. This volume contains research shaping the conversation regarding what the future may hold to protect businesses and consumers regarding the perils of digital technology.

For more information, please visit our website: www.RefractiveThinker.com

PUBLICATIONS ORDER FORM

Please send the following books from The Refractive Thinker®:

- ❏ *Volume I: An Anthology of Higher Learning*
- ❏ *Volume II: Research Methodology*
- ❏ *Volume II: Research Methodology, 2nd Edition*
- ❏ *Volume II: Research Methodology, 3rd Edition*
- ❏ *Volume III: Change Management*
- ❏ *Volume IV: Ethics, Leadership, and Globalization*
- ❏ *Volume V: Strategy in Innovation*
- ❏ *Volume VI: Post-Secondary Education*
- ❏ *Volume VII: Social Responsibility*
- ❏ *Volume VIII: Effective Business Practices*
- ❏ *Volume IX: Effective Business Practices in Leadership & Emerging Technologies*
- ❏ *Volume X: Effective Business Strategies for the Defense Industry Sector*
- ❏ *Volume XI: Women in Leadership*
- ❏ *Volume XII: Cybersecurity*
- ❏ *Volume XIII: Entrepreneurship*
- ❏ *Volume XIV: Healthcare*
- ❏ *Volume XV: Nonprofits*
- ❏ *Volume XVI: Generations*

Please contact the Refractive Thinker® Press for book prices, e-book prices, and shipping. Individual e-chapters available by author: $3.95 (plus applicable tax). www.RefractiveThinker.com

- ❏ *So You Think You Can Edit?*
- ❏ *The Expert Success Solution*
- ❏ *The Unbounded Dimensions Series*
- ❏ *Ethics, Employment Law, and Faith-Based Universities*
- ❏ *Effective Study Skills in 5 Simple Steps*
- ❏ *Technology That Tutors*
- ❏ *Siberian Husky Rescue*
- ❏ *The Consumer Learner*
- ❏ *Journey Outside the Golden Palace*
- ❏ *The Dissertation Toolbox*

Please send more FREE information:

❏ Speaking engagements   ❏ Educational seminars   ❏ Consulting

Join our mailing list:

Name: _____

Address: _____

City: _____ State: _____ Zip: _____

Telephone: _____ Email: _____

E-mail form to: **The Refractive Thinker® Press:** drcheryllentz@gmail.com

Participation in
Future Volumes of
The Refractive Thinker®

Yes, I would like to participate in:

❏ **Doctoral Volume**(s) for a specific university or organization:

Name: _____

Contact Person: _____

Telephone: _____ E-mail:_____

❏ **Specialized Volume**(s) Business or Themed:

Name: _____

Contact Person: _____

Telephone: _____ E-mail:_____

E-mail form to: The Refractive Thinker® Press
drcheryllentz@gmail.com
www.RefractiveThinker.com